The Wines of Alsace

The Wines of Alsace
A Buyer's Guide

Liz Berry

THE BODLEY HEAD
LONDON

Acknowledgements

I would like to thank all those who helped to produce this book – Jill Norman for her constant encouragement and help; Andrew and Penny Hyatt and Olivier Humbrecht, who helped taste many of the innumerable samples; Marc Kreydenweiss and Catherine Lacoste, who helped track down many fine wines from smaller producers, and provided marvellous hospitality over many visits to the region; and of course my husband Mike for arranging tastings and visits, and his grand-prix-like driving in Alsace.

As a wine merchant, I sell wines from many of the producers mentioned in this book, but as far as possible, I have tasted the wines blind for my assessments, and have tried to produce as unprejudiced a selection as possible!

A Jill Norman Book

ISBN: 0 370 31347 X
Text copyright © Liz Berry

A CIP catalogue record for this book
is available from the British Library.

Typeset by Rowland Phototypesetting Ltd
Bury St Edmunds, Suffolk
Printed in Great Britain
for the Bodley Head Ltd,
31 Bedford Square,
London WC1B 3SG
by St Edmundsbury Press Ltd
Bury St Edmunds, Suffolk

First published in 1989

CONTENTS

Introduction   6
The Appellation Contrôlée System in Alsace   15
Vintages   21
The Commercial Structure   29
How to Read an Alsace Label   33
Viticulture   37
Vinification   41
Soils   44
Varietal Labelling   46
Riesling   49
Gewurztraminer   92
Muscat   138
Tokay-Pinot Gris   154
Pinot Noir   176
Pinot Blanc   189
Sylvaner   203
Chasselas   210
Klevener de Heiligenstein   212
Kaefferkopf   215
Edelzwicker   217
Crémant d'Alsace   222
Vins de Liqueur and Vins de Paille   230
Eaux-de-vie and Fruit Liqueurs   231
Some Growers   233
Some Vineyards   245
The Confrérie St-Étienne   250
Wine Fairs   252
Bibliography   253
Index   254

INTRODUCTION

As Alsace has around 28,000 individual vineyard holdings, only 2,000 of which own over two hectares and over 1,300 of which bottle their own wine, each grower producing between six and twenty styles of wine each year, it would be impossible to do justice to all the wines produced in the Alsace region. My aim is to highlight the best and most consistent winemakers (in my opinion) within each grape variety, and to indicate the 'house style' of the wine in each case, giving a rough guide to vintages available, the price range to be expected and a personal quality rating. Wherever possible, the current vintage available has been tasted and in many cases I have also tasted several older vintages over the past few years, but it should be borne in mind that wine is a living thing and my quality ratings apply to the way I have found these wines in recent times. Over the past year, I have tasted over a thousand Alsace wines, both in London and in Alsace, and it is on these tastings that I have based this book.

HOW TO USE THE BOOK

Wines are divided into chapters by grape variety and within each chapter producers are listed alphabetically. The index includes all references to each producer.

Each entry gives a tasting note on the wine showing the style – light or heavy, delicate or powerful – a personal rating and a rough indication of optimum drinking time, measured from the date of the vintage. Vintages in brackets denote the vintages tasted for the tasting notes. A rough price guide is also given for each entry.

Pricing

Not all the wines mentioned are currently available on the UK market, and some that do come to the UK are not very widely available, but I have tried to translate the price into the price you would expect to pay by the bottle, including VAT, in an average highstreet retailer. Because of our current duty rates, this would translate roughly to mean that a wine available at the cellar door in Alsace (to the public, not to the trade), at a price of 15 FF, would sell in the UK at between £3·00 and £4·00, allowing for duty, transport, VAT and profit margin. On the other hand, because of the doubtful blessing of slower sales of Alsace wines, you would be quite likely to find vintages such as 1983 and 1985, and even older wines, on the shelves in the UK, whereas in Alsace you would mainly find 1986 and 1987 wines. I have divided the wines into six price brackets:

Up to £5	①
£5 – £8	②
£9 – £12	③
£13 – £20	④
£20 – £30	⑤
over £30	eg (£50)

Quality Rating

I have highlighted the better producers in each grape variety, and many of the better wines are illustrated with a label. In addition, the top wines have been given a star rating:

Recommended	★
Highly recommended	★★
Outstanding in its class	★★★

WHERE IS ALSACE?

It can be seen from the map of France that the Rhine separates Alsace from Germany on the east, whilst the Vosges mountains isolate the region quite effectively from the rest of France on the west, forming an 'island', and a race of people who are first and formost 'Alsaciens', rather than 'French' or 'German'. This position goes far to explain the style of wines produced and the character of the winegrowers. Many of the winegrowers owe their ancestry equally to both countries and the growers' names as well as the town names are evocative of Germany as much as of France. This isolation has resulted in a race who have kept their identity, their local customs, traditions and language, and who have a long and proud history, if a somewhat chequered one.

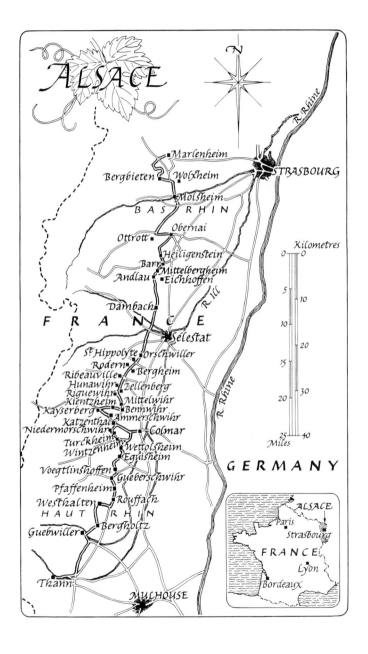

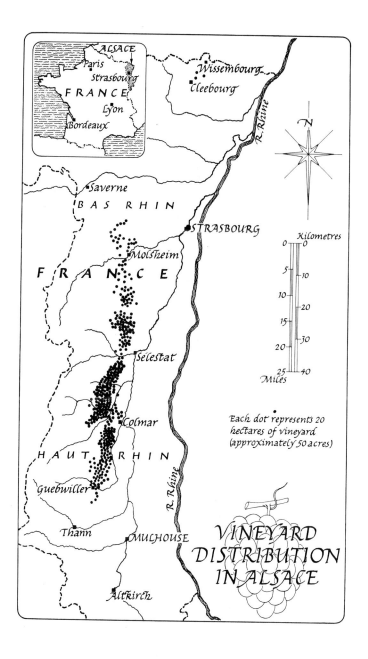

ALSACE
Paris
Strasbourg
F R A N C E
Lyon
Bordeaux

Wissembourg
Cleebourg

R. Rhine

Saverne

B A S   R H I N

STRASBOURG

F R A N C E

Molsheim

Selestat

Colmar

H A U T   R H I N

Guebwiller

Thann

MULHOUSE

Altkirch

R. Rhine

Kilometres
0 — 0
5 — 10
10 — 20
15 — 30
20 — 40
25
Miles

Each dot represents 20
hectares of vineyard
(approximately 50 acres)

VINEYARD
DISTRIBUTION
IN ALSACE

Alsace has two départements, Bas Rhin and Haut Rhin. Bas Rhin, from Wissemborg in the north to Selestat, is by far the smaller region, and less highly regarded. Its slightly more northerly situation often gives wines that are lighter in alcohol and body, with a less powerful, more ethereal character. The acidity may be more noticeable, and this region therefore succeeds better with the leaner-structured varieties, Pinot Blanc, Sylvaner, Riesling, which in an exceptionally well-placed site can produce exciting wines, with steeliness and vivacity, and long ageing potential. The Bas Rhin is less successful with the fatter, fleshier varieties, and Tokay-Pinot Gris and Gewurztraminer can sometimes be a little lacking in power and concentration. There are only 12 Grand Cru sites in the Bas Rhin compared with 35 in the Haut Rhin. These sites, however, can produce wines of outstanding character, and fully deserve their place amongst the best wines of Alsace. I have found the wines of Kastelberg, Wiebelsberg, and Altenberg de Bergheim to be of particular note. The Haut Rhin from Selestat down to Thann contains most of the well known names in Alsace, and has a far larger choice of top quality vineyard sites. The wines are generally richer, fuller-bodied and more powerful. On certain sites they can be almost clumsy and over-alcoholic. The Haut Rhin contains most of the specialist wine villages, and generally produces the bulk of Vendange Tardive wines, although some very good ones are also produced in the Bas Rhin.

HISTORY

Vines were introduced around the time of the Romans. In the twelfth century Alsace wines were well-known and regarded, with specific vineyards, such as Kastelberg, Moenchberg, Niedermorschwihr, Hengst and Rangen, renowned for higher quality. In this period vineyards were largely cultivated by the church, which owned large tracts of land. As in other parts of France, the monks were largely responsible for increasing the quality of viticulture and vinification and for choosing the best vineyard sites. In the thirteenth century, Alsace wines were considered to be amongst Europe's finest wines. They were well known in England, where they were sold under the name of Ryneys, Rinoys or Renois, meaning Rhine wine, or as

Aussey, Osey or Aussai, meaning Alsace. In 1300, 172 villages were named as producing the best wine in Alsace.

In the fourteenth century the names of noble grape varieties started to appear, edicts were passed limiting the varieties which could be planted on the best sites and forbidding the culture of less good varieties. These were years of prosperity for the region, as the Rhine became more navigable and was an important waterway, with Strasbourg an important port for the export of wines and the import of spices.

In the Middle Ages, wine commerce had to be carried out via the offices of an intermediary, who would match buyer and seller, taking a commission on sales. In Alsace, this role was practised by a 'gourmet'. Each town and village in Alsace boasted one or several gourmets, who would often combine the role with that of innkeeper, enabling them to house and feed their prospective clients. A bell on the town hall roof announced the arrival of a customer to the village, the gourmet would take the purchaser around the cellars of his region and would be knowledgeable of the different qualities and crus of each producer, together with prices, and the quantities available. All transactions were entered in the local *Registre de Gourmettage*, and the gourmet's commission consisted of both wine and money. The *Stichwein*, two litres per cask sold (a cask contained 1,000 litres) was paid by the seller, while the cash payment, the *Stichgeld*, was paid by both purchaser and vendor. A gourmet was not allowed to sell the wines from his own cellar, except through the services of another gourmet, and the system safeguarded the trade well against any malpractices. The gourmet would often make recommendations to the *vigneron* as to how he could improve his wines or his vineyards. In 1790 liberty of commerce was introduced, and it was no longer necessary to use gourmets as intermediaries. The system died out and the role was taken over to some extent by that of *courtier*, or merchant.

During the Thirty Years War, between 1618 and 1648, many of the vineyards were destroyed and records show that whereas 12 million bottles of wine were exported from Colmar between 1530 and 1590, the figure had fallen to around 2 million bottles between 1630 and 1690. By 1720, England had ceased to buy any wine at all from Alsace. There were many more vineyard owners, and greedy *vignerons* planted much of the land on the plain, hoping to profit from the high reputation of Alsace wines grown on more favourable hillside sites. In some parts the area under vine doubled or even trebled, and only the top sites still owned by the clergy maintained their high reputation for quality. The strict rule before the Thirty Years War had been that wines on the plain were for 'own drinking', and were not for selling. In 1731, there were insufficient crops, the price of grain rose, and pasture for animals was becoming scarce, as the area under vine was rapidly increasing. The authorities banned further planting of unsuitable sites and warned against a loss of market for the good wines, as many of the newly planted areas were producing poor quality wines, prejudicial to the region and to the producers' reputation. The law was hard to enforce, through lack of personnel and influx of people from outside the region, and was restated in 1766, with threats of fines of up to 3,000 livres. Over-production followed, especially when taxes were increased, and Holland was at war with Louis XIV, depriving Alsace of an important trade outlet.

The yields had also increased, from an average of 41 hectolitres per hectare in 1786/88 to an average of 58 hectolitres per hectare in 1826/7. The Napoleonic wars provided a good market, as troops stationed in Alsace consumed large quantities of wine. The Mayor of Wintzenheim observed that 40,000 soldiers stationed in Alsace could consume at least 40,000 litres of wine a day. With the French Revolution, larger estates were split up and redistributed. The area under vine increased from around 23,000 hectares in 1808 to over 30,000 hectares in 1828. Prices fell dramatically for several reasons. Transport had become easier for the inexpensive wines of the Midi, which competed for the internal market, and in 1828 the German frontiers closed to trade. The beer market was also starting to develop in the region. Prices fell by as much as half or two-thirds, to around 10 francs for a measure of fifty litres before the closure of the German frontier, and were down to a mere 4 francs a measure after the closure. The cellars in 1828 were full of the wines from 1826 and 1825, both large crops, and in spite of the low prices, stocks remained very high. There were many protests in the area, both peaceful and otherwise, and winemaking had become uneconomical. By 1852 the plantations on the plain were being replaced by other crops and the area had shrunk to 11,421 hectares, and to 10,126 hectares in 1861. The vineyards on the foothills of the Vosges improved the quality of their wines, by replacing varietals and by new improved methods of viticulture, and their reputation increased.

In 1871 Alsace was annexed by the Germans, who already had fine vineyard sites of their own and who used the wines of Alsace for blending purposes. They authorised such hitherto frowned-upon practices as chaptalisation (the addition of sugar to the must), and *mouillage* (the addition of sugar and water, to dilute the over-acidity of rather poor wine). The Palatinate wines were cheaper but of lower quality, and growers were encouraged to aim for quantity rather than quality.

At the end of the nineteenth century, after the vineyards had been decimated by phylloxera and oidium, the Germans forbade the replanting of noble varieties, and ordered hybrids, resistant to these problems and producing a large yield, to be planted in their place. Only a few *vignerons* resisted and replanted with noble vines, whilst the majority were content to produce trouble-free, large crops of uninteresting wine, which had a ready market as blending wine. At the beginning of this century, varieties planted included Bouquetraube, Abordant Blanc, Chasselas, Knipperlé, Goldriesling, Müller Thurgau and various hybrids, with only small patches of 'noble' or top quality varietals. The prices had sunk to a new low by 1910, because of the general lack of quality.

In 1918, after the First World War, Alsace returned to France, and the hybrids started to be uprooted and replaced by small acreage of the noble varieties, planted only in the better sites. Only one-third of the vineyards were of the noble varieties at this time, the remaining two-thirds comprising Sylvaner, Chasselas and lesser varieties. Knowledge of viticulture had improved, methods of resisting diseases and pests had been developed, and the vines were replanted on a more scientific basis. The French law of 1919 stated that the vineyard region should comprise the area of 'usages locaux, constants et loyaux' – the 'traditional' sites, which were still somewhat vague at this time. Many champions of quality wine started to buy vineyard land at this time and to plant the best sites with noble varieties. The area under vines was now about half the size it had been at the end of the nineteenth century.

During the Second World War, Alsace was once again overrun by the Germans, who much enjoyed drinking up the finer wines of the region! Export was impossible and growers faced some very lean years. In 1945, when the first statutes were laid down towards the future granting of Appellation Contrôlée status, the growers were limited in varietals, yield, and viticultural practices, without the benefit of Appellation Contrôlée on the label. They had not yet 'got their act together' sufficiently to be granted Appellation Contrôlée, and many growers still had large acreages of trouble-free, large-yielding, but poor-tasting grapes. The English market started cautiously buying small quantities of Alsace wines: German wines were understandably unpopular and the merchants hoped to wean their customers over to the style of Alsace wines. However, the confusion which still reigns today made it hard to market the wines: the winemakers' names are Germanic, the bottle shape is Germanic, the grape varieties sound Germanic, and the wine was often sold as 'French Rhine Wine'! The traditional green flute bottle was officially adopted in 1959, and a decree stated that all Alsace wines must be bottled in these bottles. (From 1972 all wines had also to be bottled in the region of production, as a further safeguard against fraud.)

In the 1960s there was still only a very limited market for Alsace wines, which had therefore to sell at low prices. Vineyard land was also at a very low premium, and the 1960s and 1970s were the period for astute growers to take advantage and buy up parcels of the best land at very low prices. In the 1970s, because of local pressure from growers, the decision was taken to enlarge the area of plantation by some 1,000 hectares, of which around 600 hectares were on flat land, of poor quality for vine production. However, there were also growers buying up neglected parcels of 'hard to work' vineyards on steeper slopes, in the better sites. As a result, there is a large acreage of young vines in Alsace, spread between poor, medium and top quality sites. There is also a large divergence in price and quality, dependent upon whether the winemaker has opted for quality or quantity.

THE APPELLATION CONTRÔLÉE
SYSTEM IN ALSACE

Appellation Contrôlée is a system to control the quality of wine within a region. The rules lay down the zone covered, the varieties that may be planted, the maximum yields, the methods of cultivation and winemaking and the degree of alcohol which must be obtained. In addition, Alsace has opted to lay down the bottle shape and to insist that all wines must be bottled in the region of production. The different ACs in Alsace are:

Alsace or Vin d'Alsace
Alsace or Vin d'Alsace followed by one of the following:
    Gewurztraminer
    Riesling
    Tokay-Pinot Gris
    Muscat
    Pinot Blanc
    Klevner or Clevner
    Sylvaner
    Chasselas or Gutedel
    Auxerrois
    Pinot Noir
    Edelzwicker
    Clairet de Schillerwein (rosé)
    Klevener de Heiligenstein
Alsace Grand Cru
Alsace Grand Cru followed by a vineyard name (see Appendix)
    Crémant d'Alsace

Appellation Contrôlée was granted in 1962. At that time, Grand Cru was used for certain varieties reaching a higher alcoholic degree than for the basic wine, with no mention of vineyard sites. In 1971 an amendment was passed allowing the name of a particular vineyard or village to appear on the label if the wine was from one of the recommended varieties:– Riesling, Gewurztraminer, Muscat, Pinot Blanc, Tokay-Pinot Gris, Sylvaner or Chasselas. In 1975 Grand Cru was changed from its original meaning, to indicate one of 25 individual sites. A further 22 sites were added in 1986. In

1976, Crémant d'Alsace was granted Appellation Contrôlée.

Alsace wines must have a minimum potential alcohol of 8·5°, with a maximum yield of 100 hectolitres per hectare. Grand Cru wines must have a minimum potential alcohol of 10° or 11°, depending on the variety, with the maximum yield reduced to 70 hectolitres per hectare.

The system of pruning is also laid down, allowing a maximum of 12 buds per square metre to be left on the vines. The *Ban de Vendanges*, or date to commence picking, is also strictly controlled, the Comité Régional d'Experts des Vins d'Alsace announcing the starting date, which will differ according to the grape variety, and to whether the wine is destined for the manufacture of Crémant.

There is also a new level of Appellation under discussion, an 'intermediate' band, which will cover whole villages and areas, probably accounting for 80 per cent or more of the total vineyards. It will not be a *terroir* appellation, in the manner of the Grands Crus, as producers will be allowed to blend between vineyards, and will probably be called Alsace Villages, or Coteaux d'Alsace, or some such name. Growers rather fancied the name Premier Cru, but this is not likely to be permitted. It is seen by many to be a purely political move, to upgrade vineyards belonging to those growers who do not have any Grand Cru sites, and are now saying 'me too'.

An additional Appellation is available for late picked grapes of certain varietals, under the denomination Vendanges Tardives, or Sélection de Grains Nobles.

ALSACE GRAND CRU

For centuries there has been a tradition of naming the individual vineyard slopes in Alsace, and wines from certain vineyards have always fetched a premium. The best vineyards will give a unique *goût de terroir*, or character imparted by the soil to the wines, in addition to the varietal character imparted by the grape variety, providing that the yields are strictly controlled. The words 'Grand Cru' on an Alsace label originally designated a wine that was a little richer in flavour, from grapes with a higher must weight, but on 20 November 1975 a decree was issued, limiting the yield for Grand Cru wines to 70 hectolitres per hectare, only from the following four grape varieties: Riesling, Muscat, Gewurztraminer and Pinot Gris. Riesling and Muscat had to attain a minimum natural must weight of 170 grams per litre of sugar and reach a minimum of 10° after fermentation, whilst the minimum limit for Gewurztraminer and Pinot Gris was 187 grams per litre of sugar, with a minimum of 11°. The grapes must all come from the same vintage and both the vintage and the variety must be mentioned on the label as well as the words 'Grand Cru'. The wines have to be subjected to a tasting panel, as well as undergoing analytical tests. A list of *lieux-dits*, or vineyard names was drawn up and these could also appear on the label of Grand Cru wines.

On 23 November 1983 a list of 25 vineyards was drawn up, after analysis of their geological structure and aspect, and in November 1985 a further 22 vineyards were added to the list.

From 1983, Grand Cru could no longer be used merely to denote a higher alcohol content, as in the original Appellation Contrôlée law. At present, around 2·5% of the production of Alsace wine is declared as AC Grand Cru. A larger percentage is under vine, but not declared. Some Alsace houses prefer to commercialise their wines under other labels, or wish to blend between vineyards for a better overall wine, or simply do not wish to sell their wines as Grand Cru. Grand Cru vineyards account for some 435 hectares of vines. Some highly regarded sites in Alsace have decided not to apply for Grand Cru status, whilst others have applied but have not as yet been considered of sufficient quality.

The current list of Grand Cru Vineyards comprises:

Vineyard	*Village or Villages*
Altenberg de Bergbieten	Bergbieten
Altenberg de Bergheim	Bergheim
Altenberg de Wolxheim	Wolxheim
Brand	Turckheim
Elchberg	Eguisheim
Engelberg	Dahlenheim
Franckstein	Dambach la Ville
Froehn	Zellenberg
Geisberg	Ribeauvillé
Gloeckelberg	Rodern, Saint-Hippolyte
Goldert	Gueberschwihr
Hatschbourg	Hattstatt, Voegtlinshoffen

Vineyard	Village or Villages
Hengst	Winzenheim
Kanzlerberg	Bergheim
Kastelberg	Andlau
Kessler	Guebwiller
Kirchberg de Barr	Barr
Kirchberg de Ribeauvillé	Ribeauvillé
Kitterlé	Guebwiller
Mambourg	Sigolsheim
Mandelberg	Mittelwihr
Markrain	Bennwihr
Moenchberg	Andlau, Eichhoffen
Muenchberg	Nothalten
Ollwiller	Wuenheim
Osterberg	Ribeauvillé
Pfersigberg	Eguisheim
Pfingstberg	Orschwihr
Rangen	Thann, Vieux Thann
Rosacker	Hunawihr
Saering	Guebwiller
Schlossberg	Kayserberg, Kientzheim
Schoenenberg	Riquewihr
Sommerberg	Niedermorschwihr, Katzenthal
Sonnenglanz	Beblenheim
Spiegel	Bergholz, Guebwiller
Sporen	Riquewihr
Steinert	Pfaffenheim
Steingrubler	Wettolsheim
Steinkolz	Marlenheim
Traeletenberg	Orschwiller
Vorbourg	Rouffach, Westhalten
Wiebelsberg	Andlau
Wineck-Schlossberg	Katzenthal
Winzenberg	Blienschwiller
Zinnkoepflé	Westhalten, Soultzmatt
Zotzenberg	Mittelbergheim

The latest 22 recruits have not so far been entirely delimited. The growers and the authorities have to agree the exact boundaries within which Grand Cru grapes may be grown. Until that time, it is possible to find these vineyard sites named both with and without the mention 'Grand Cru', dependent upon whether the grower has followed Grand Cru regulations, and declared his intention to the authorities, submitting the wines for tasting and analysis.

VENDANGE TARDIVE, SÉLECTION DE GRAINS NOBLES

Vendange Tardive wines are wines that are late-picked, with therefore more sugar and more potential alcohol. They vary from medium-sweet to dry, dependent upon how much of the sugar has fermented out. Sélection de Grains Nobles wines are even later picked, usually with *botrytis cinerea*, or noble rot, a fungus that attacks ripe grapes late in the season, piercing the grape's skin with its filaments, and producing a grape with less water content, therefore with a higher concentration of sugar and acidity. It also alters some of the chemical constituents in the juice, giving a very individual and special flavour to the resultant wine. Wines made from botrytis-affected grapes often have a raisiny, almost antiseptic smell and taste, with higher volatility and more glycerol, giving a smooth but almost bitter-sweet flavour. The wines labelled Seléction de Grains Nobles will be medium-sweet to very sweet.

Some top producers have been making these wines for many years, but only in vintages that merited this style of wine. Formerly, these wines were sometimes labelled 'Auslese' or 'Beerenauslese', but the need of a separate identity from German wines has led to the use of the current French terms. These wines were considered a speciality, a happy accident of the weather, when growers would leave a small parcel of exceptionally ripe grapes after the main harvest, and keep their fingers crossed for warm, dry weather. A rainstorm could wipe out this crop, as could hungry birds, or even itinerant grape-pickers, believing that these grapes were not required! In 1976 quite a number of growers made Vendange Tardive wines, and other winemakers started to adopt this practice as a new form of winemaking. The traditional makers of these wines, notably Jean Hugel, one of the foremost pioneers, felt that the time was coming for some regulations to cover this style of wine, to prevent abuses, and in 1984 legal standards were officially drawn up. The requirements are as follows:

The local authorities have to be informed of the intention to make a Vendange Tardive wine before the grapes are picked, and a register is kept of the grower's name and the size of the parcel of land.

The wines may not be chaptalised or enriched.

The wines must come 100% from one of the four authorised grapes: Gewurztraminer, Riesling, Muscat or Tokay-Pinot Gris.

The minimum must weights are laid down.

The wines must be of a single vintage and must be vintage dated on the label.

The finished wines must undergo a chemical analysis, and pass a tasting panel, who usually taste in March/May a year from the harvest, after the wines are in bottle, or ready to bottle.

The minimum must weights laid down are:

Vendange Tardive

Riesling	220 gms/lit sugar (95° oechsle)	12·9 potential alcohol
Muscat	220 gms/lit sugar (95° oechsle)	12·9° potential alcohol
Gewurztraminer	243 gms/lit sugar (105° oechsle)	14·3° potential alcohol
Tokay-Pinot Gris	243 gms/lit sugar (105° oechsle)	14·3 potential alcohol

Sélection de Grains Nobles

Riesling	256 gms/lit sugar (110° oechsle)	15·1° potential alcohol
Muscat	256 gms/lit sugar (110° oechsle)	15·1° potential alcohol
Gewurztraminer	279 gms/lit sugar (120° oechsle)	16·4° potential alcohol
Tokay-Pinot Gris	279 gms/lit sugar (120° oechsle)	16·4° potential alcohol

Because of the quality of the 1983 and 1985 vintages, many growers are now making this style of wine. The wines need long ageing and do not show at their best until five to 10 years of age, and often much longer. As the yields are so small, and the risks in producing the wines so great, the prices are high, and consumers can only fully justify these prices by laying the wines down until they show at their best.

In practice, there is only a small quantity of late-picked Riesling, and almost no Muscat, except in occasional very ripe years, such as 1983. The majority of Vendange Tardive wines come from Gewurztraminer, followed by Tokay.

Since the minimum oechsle levels were laid down, many growers will have a stab at producing a late-picked wine if they stand any chance, since they can obtain a much higher price for the wine, and many declarations are made in the hope that the grape must will scrape the necessary degree of sugar when the inspector makes his tests. On the other hand, there are many wines from top producers where the oechsle levels are well in excess of the minimum criteria. For this reason, do not buy on price alone, and do not expect the same pleasure from a supermarket Vendange Tardive as from one which costs five times as much!

'Vendanges Tardives' can be written in the plural or in the singular, some growers arguing that the picking is in fact a series of pickings, or *vendanges*.

VINTAGES

In the UK, most Alsace wines on sale will have a vintage on the label. (In many French supermarkets the less expensive wines will not bother: their turnover is large, and the wine will probably come from the most recent vintage available.) All Vendange Tardive and Sélection de Grains Nobles wines must by law state the vintage. It has long been considered that as Alsace wines are fresh and aromatic in character, the consumer should seek the youngest vintage available, as the wine will lose its character and freshness if kept too long. This is to some extent true of the lesser wines, but the vintage is far more significant than a mere 'drink by' date.

The Alsace region lies at a latitude of between 47·8° and 49° North, in north-east France. The winters here are generally bitterly cold, but spring can be mild and warm, with warm spring winds to melt the snows and the Vosges mountain to shelter the region from cold winds. The rainfall is one of the lowest in France, around 500 to 700 mm per year, because of the shelter afforded by the mountains. (The summits of the Vosges receive an average of 2,000 mm.) As many of the vineyards are on south, south-east and south-west facing slopes, there are many well sheltered sun-traps ideal for vine-growing. The effect of these sheltered slopes has been demonstrated, to show that the temperature in the middle of a slope may be one to one-and-a-half degrees warmer than at the top or bottom of the slope. Most of the best vineyards in Alsace are therefore planted on slopes, at an altitude of between 250 and 350 metres, and these sites will be less affected in a bad vintage than the flatter, less sheltered sites on the plain.

On average, Alsace produces maybe one vintage in ten that is poor, maybe two below average, three average-to-good, two to three very good, and one or two excellent.

Late frosts in the spring can cause poor flowering and therefore a small crop or a crop containing a proportion of unripe, malformed grapes. Lack of sunshine during the summer and autumn can result in poor ripening, and rain in autumn can dilute the flavour whilst increasing the quantity. Warm, damp weather can cause rot, producing a taste of mildew in the finished wine.

In a year where any (or all) of these problems are present, the role of the winemaker is much more significant and a good winemaker can influence the quality of the wine he produces by up to 90% in a poor year, whereas in a good year any competent winemaker has the raw materials with which to produce a good wine. For this reason vintage charts should only be used as an indication of the general style and quality of the year. Used in conjunction with this guide, it is to be remembered that the best winemakers will only put their name on a wine which they consider of sufficient quality, and lesser years can often provide bargains and very attractive, well-made drinking wines.

Keeping ability will also be dependent upon the soil (alluvial soils generally giving wines with poor keeping qualities), the yield and the style of wine made.

1988

Until the early autumn, the quality of the vintage could have been very fine, but unfortunately heavy rain just before the start of picking diluted the quality and increased the quantity, quickly leading to rot in the less well-drained vineyards. The successful wines are generally clean, balanced, with good weight of fruit, much in the style of 1986. There are some late-picked wines, both Vendange Tardive and Séléction des Grains Nobles, and although there was some noble rot, many will be made from healthy, extra-ripe grapes, where the fine late autumn weather has concentrated the sugar content. Overall rating: 7/10

1987

The weather throughout the growing season was variable, with high rainfall, and so the wines are generally average, the importance of the producer coming to the fore. The quantity was a little lower than 1986, especially in the Bas Rhin. Wines are generally well-balanced, with good acidity and good structure, and should age well. There are some very good Vendange Tardive wines, and a very small quantity of Sélection de Grains Nobles. Overall rating: 7/10

1986

Mixed weather throughout the summer caused some rot in most areas and selection was necessary. The overall crop was large and some wines will be rather dilute in flavour. The late autumn weather was perfect for the formation of botrytis and some very good Vendange Tardive and Sélection de Grains Nobles have been produced. The wines should age well, particularly the Rieslings, which have very good structure and acidity. Overall rating: 7/10

1985

A summer with good, slow, even ripening of the grapes produced some superb results, and in general wines from 1985 have very good balance, with higher alcohol levels than usual, but still with good acidity. It was a dry vintage and some vines suffered a little from drought at the end of the season, especially on lighter, well-drained soils. Overall, the crop was smaller than average, especially for Muscat and Gewurztraminer. The late autumn weather was warm and dry and a large quantity of late-harvest wines have been made. There was, however, practically no botrytis in this vintage, the sugar levels being attained by overripeness rather than noble rot, and some of the finished wines rather lacking that extra dimension. There are some excellent Vendange Tardive wines, however, especially in Tokay and Riesling, and the wines overall should last well, the better wines keeping until the beginning of the next century. Overall rating: 9/10

1984

1984 was a very difficult vintage, with little sun and a lot of rot on the vines. Because of uneven flowering, many bunches of grapes at harvest time had a mixture of ripe, unripe and rotten grapes, and very careful selection was necessary. The minimum alcohol levels were officially lowered and many wines are thin, with a high acidity and lacking in ripeness. Many wines also have a very marked taste of the vintage; an aroma and flavour of acacia honey, in some cases with a touch of oxidation. In spite of this, the best producers made some very acceptable wines by careful selection. This is a vintage where one should buy from reliable producers only. Overall rating: 3/10

1983

A hot summer with little rain produced grapes with high sugar levels and therefore wines with higher alcohol than usual. In spite of this, acidity levels are generally good, often higher than in 1976 or 1971. Some of the lesser varietals, such as Sylvaners, produced lovely big, spicy wines, which are still very attractive. Muscats were generally a little too fat and overblown, and many are now rather oily and lacking in varietal character. Tokays and Gewurztraminers are wonderful; many are still too young and should be bought for laying down while they are still available, as should good quality Rieslings, which will carry on until the next century. Different producers vary in their opinion as to whether their 1983 or 1985 wines were better, but the overall agreement is that '1983 is the wine for tasting, and 1985 the wine for drinking with food'. There are some excellent late-picked wines, which are still available, and have lovely balance of rich botrytis fruit and acidity. Overall rating: 9/10

1982

This was a very large vintage, consequently many wines are a little diluted and are ageing rapidly. The colour is often quite advanced and many wines have a soft, developed apricot flavour. Some wines from the best producers, and some Vendange Tardive wines, should still improve, but overall these are wines for drinking now. Overall rating: 5/10

1981

Some well-balanced wines were produced, with good sugar levels, but with lower acidity than usual. Most wines are for drinking now, but the best Rieslings will still keep, as will the few late-picked wines of this vintage. Overall rating: 7/10

1980

Most wines were very lightweight, with little concentration and should have been drunk by now. Overall rating: 5/10

1979

A large quantity of good quality wines, often with quite low acidity, and therefore better drunk up now. Some top Rieslings are still excellent, as are better Tokays and Gewurztraminers. Overall rating: 7/10

1978

A small crop, with some very good wines, particularly in Rieslings and Tokays. Some wines had quite high acidity, but this has helped the better wines to last. Top quality Rieslings and Tokays can still be kept. Overall rating: 6/10

1977

Quite a large crop, but many wines were rather thin, with high acidity. Many wines have developed a quite oily flavour. Some good Rieslings will still keep, but most wines should be drunk up. Overall rating: 4/10

1976

An excellent vintage of rich, powerful, concentrated wines, often with less acidity than usual. Wines from vineyards whose heavier soil retained moisture through the summer had sufficient acidity, but some wines from vineyards on lighter, drier soil can lack acidity. Many of the top wines from this vintage have gone through a somewhat aggressive, hard phase, but now seem to be coming out of that stage and maturing well. There was an abundance of late-picked wines in 1976, many producers making Vendange Tardive and Sélection de Grains Nobles wines for the first time. The best wines will still need further keeping and top wines should be laid down for several years yet. Overall rating: 9+/10

1975

A normal size vintage, which produced some good quality wines, especially in Riesling and Gewurztraminer. Overall rating: 7/10

1974

A small vintage, with little Gewurztraminer. Some Rieslings are still lasting well. Overall rating: 6/10

1973

The largest vintage in the 1970s, with some excellent quality wines, which have lasted well and are still surprisingly fresh. Most better quality wines from this vintage will have lasted well. Overall rating: 8/10

1972

Very mean, unripe, 'green' – tasting wines, most of which have stayed mean and oily. Occasional Rieslings have lasted well, where the acidity is not too dominant. Overall Rating: 3/10

1971

The smallest vintage in the 1970s, producing some excellent wines, with good fruit acid balance, and a classic gunflint flavour. The top wines of Tokay, Riesling and Gewurztraminer have lasted well and many could still be kept longer. Overall Rating: 9/10

1970

A large crop of soft, attractive wines, rather lacking in acidity. Many wines will have become rather oily by now, but there are still very good Rieslings to be found. Overall rating: 6/10

1969

Earthy, buttery, ripe wines, with good sugar levels, and quite good acidity. The top Rieslings, Gewurztraminers and Tokays are still keeping well. Overall rating: 8+/10

1968

Very poor vintage, unripe wines. Overall rating: 1/10

1967

Two-thirds of the vintage was poor, the other third was outstanding, depending on whether picking was before or after the autumn rains. Some exceptional wines, very well-balanced, still lasting well. Some superb late-picked wines were produced, many of which are still in their infancy and will live for many years. Overall rating: 9/10

1966

A very good vintage, well-balanced wines. The top Rieslings and Tokays are still good. Overall rating: 7/10

1965

A very poor vintage, unripe, thin wines. Overall rating: 0/10

1964

An excellent vintage of very ripe, well balanced wines, many of which are still lasting well. Overall rating: 8+/10

1963

A large vintage of often rather dilute wines. Overall rating: 3/10

1962

A small vintage of very good quality, well-balanced wines. Overall rating: 7/10

1961

An excellent vintage of powerfully-structured, well-balanced wines. The top wines of this vintage are still superb. Overall rating: 9/10

1960

Lighter weight wines, well-balanced, but many now a little tired. Some very good Rieslings and Gewurztraminers can still be found. Overall rating: 7/10

1959

Superb quality vintage, wines high in sugar, and therefore alcohol, sometimes a little low in acidity. Some superb quality Vendange Tardive wines, which have still lasted well. Overall rating: 9/10

Ratings for the older vintages are unfortunately culled largely from other people's experience, and little enough from my own tasting notes. It is very hard to find older vintages than 1959, although the Oenothèque belonging to the Confrérie St. Étienne has wines going back to 1834!

1958	6/10	*1928*	9/10
1957	7/10	*1927*	5/10
1956	5/10	*1926*	7/10

1955	8/10	*1925*	4/10
1954	7/10	*1924*	6/10
1953	9/10	*1923*	6/10
1952	7/10	*1922*	6/10
1951	2/10	*1921*	7/10
1950	7/10	*1920*	4/10
1949	7/10	*1919*	6/10
1948	7/10	*1918*	3/10
1947	9/10	*1917*	6/10
1946	5/10	*1916*	3/10
1945	8/10	*1915*	6/10
1944	2/10	*1914*	5/10
1943	7+/10	*1913*	2/10
1942	7/10	*1912*	4/10
1941	5/10	*1911*	7/10
1940	3/10	*1910*	3/10
1939	3/10	*1909*	3/10
1938	7/10	*1908*	5/10
1937	7+/10	*1907*	6/10
1936	5/10	*1906*	4/10
1935	4/10	*1905*	6/10
1934	6/10	*1904*	6/10
1933	5/10	*1903*	5/10
1932	5/10	*1902*	3/10
1931	5/10	*1901*	3/10
1930	3/10	*1900*	7/10
1929	8/10		

THE COMMERCIAL STRUCTURE

The wines are made and marketed in Alsace by *négociants*, co-operatives and individual grower/winemakers. Each year, around 10,000 declarations are made of intent to harvest, many of these grapes being destined for the co-operatives or *négociants*. However, between 1,300 and 2,000 growers bottle and sell their own wine, over 80 per cent of the total volume being in the hands of a mere 175 of these. There are 17 co-operatives, and 65 *négociants*. Around 40 per cent of all the wine is produced by *négociants*, around 30/35 per cent by co-operatives, and the remaining 25/30 per cent is produced and marketed by individual growers. A large amount of Alsace wine is sold at the winery door, to tourists and to visiting wine-lovers who travel to the region to pick up supplies. Germany provides the largest export market, although the bulk of its purchases consists of lower priced, lower quality wine. France provides a very large home market, with Alsace wines accounting for 40 per cent of domestic AC dry white wine consumption. England and America are only very small consumers at present, although figures are gradually increasing. A good two-thirds of all wine exported comes from the *négociants*, most of the remainder from the co-operatives, and only around 5 per cent from individual growers. It is interesting to study the structure of the three groups.

NÉGOCIANTS

A *négociant* is a commercial wine company. Most of the large *négociants* own vineyards, but the name *négociant* rather than *propriétaire* is used by any company or individual who does not deal exclusively in the produce of their own vines, but who also buys in grapes or wine. Before the advent of the co-operatives, growers sold their wine to the *négociants*, or vinified and sold it themselves. Now they have the choice between the three. The grapes are purchased according to varietal and must-weight, some varieties fetching far higher prices than others. The *négociant* vinifies the wine and markets it. The grower has the advantage of a lump sum for his grapes and none of the financial worries involved in sales. As a *négociant* generally operates on a larger scale than a *propriétaire*, he has a much larger quantity of wine to sell, and does not face the problems of continuity of the smaller grower. He can set up agencies in each country to sell his wine, giving the wines a wide distribution throughout restaurants, hotels and shops. He has money available for publicity, and can ensure a niche in the market place. He can also tailor his wines to his market more easily than the grower and produce different cuvées of each variety to suit the style and price required. He is large enough to take on 'own label' wine production for supermarkets, and has the raw materials available to produce top price and quality blends for fine wine buyers, as well as inexpensive wines for the lower end of the market. Most *négociants* will produce a reserve quality as well as a basic quality and many will also produce small quantities of very special top quality wines for the connoisseur. The top cuvées will generally be produced from their own vineyards, where they have more control over the yield and quality of the grapes and the picking date. A disadvantage of buying from growers is that they will usually pick the grapes as early as possible, to avoid any possibility of losing the crop through bad weather. They will probably also make as high a yield as possible, to get more money. *Négociants* will often try to have long term relationships with growers, so that they are able to advise them on yield and vineyard care. The grapes are generally paid for in instalments, often four instalments of 25 per cent, or five of 20 percent over the course of a year. The growers are free to sell part of their crop and vinify the remainder, if they so wish. Often, with the co-operatives, it is all or nothing! Some *négociants*, and indeed some growers and even co-operatives, sell under more than one label. This way they can give exclusivity on different markets to different distributors. With two or more names they can also market their own wines from family-owned vineyards as *propriétaire-viticulteur* and buy in and process grapes from outside the *domaine* under a different label, provided that separate premises and separate companies are used for the two. *Négociants'* sales account for some 40 per cent of the overall market and many of the larger *négociants* produce 30 or more different styles of wine every year.

CO-OPERATIVES

A co-operative is a society owned and managed by its own members. The first Alsace co-operative was founded just after 1900, as a means of storing surplus wines and thus regulating the price. The next co-operatives were set up to share wine-making equipment and skills between members, with the idea of making wine to sell to the *négociants*. As the *négociants* did not buy, they turned their activities to bottling and selling their own wine. This was after the Second World War. Many growers in Alsace do not have sufficient means to vinify, bottle and sell their own wine, and the co-operative provided an alternative to selling to the *négociant*. Most small growers will have a job during the day and tend to their vines in the evenings and weekends. For them the co-operative means a chance to have more of a say in the way their wines are made, and a steady annual income, without the financial worries of marketing and selling the wine. The standard of technology and winemaking is often extremely high, as the co-operatives have the funding for the most modern equipment, and can hire the necessary expertise, or find it amongst their members. As with the *négociants*, their size enables them to compete on price and to find the necessary funds for marketing and promotion of their wines. The disadvantages may be that the growers take less care with their crop, as with crops intended for the *négociants*, than they would do if it were sold under their own name. Grapes will be picked at the earliest opportunity, with the largest permitted yield, as the crop is seen merely as an income, without regard to the art of winemaking. But the growers may have to wait longer for their money, as payments may depend on sales, and they may have to contract their whole crop for a number of years in order to join. There are now 17 co-operatives, with around 2,600 members, and they account for 30 per cent to 35 per cent of the production.

PROPRIÉTAIRES-VITICULTEURS, VIGNERONS, MANIPULANTS

A *propriétaire-viticulteur* or a *vigneron* is a grower who owns his own land, vinifies and sells his own wine, without buying in any grapes or wines from outside his own *domaine*. The land may be rented from someone else, but if it is under the control of the grower, who tends the vines, picks the grapes, makes and sells the wine, then it counts as his own for this purpose. The word *exploitant* or *manipulant* may occasionally be met in this case. Many *propriétaire-viticulteurs* are very small, the majority selling their own wine have less than 10 hectares of land. Even the smallest grower will produce six to ten different wines every year. Most growers will have a particular forte with two or three varieties and the quality may be less 'all round' than from a *négociant*. The advantages are that a small grower will produce a wine that is often more individual in character, coming from a particular site, and expressing the grower's style and character. The best growers are fanatically meticulous in their winemaking, restricting their vines to very small yields and producing top quality wines from the best parcels. The skill of a grower is paramount: small is not always beautiful, and not every grower has the skill or knowledge to produce top quality wines. The grower has less finance available for updating equipment and may be less in touch with recent advances in technology than a larger firm. Marketing is also more difficult, as quantities are more limited, and the grower has only himself, and his family, to act as vinegrower, winemaker, cellarman, accountant and salesman. Some of the most exciting wines in Alsace today are being produced by *propriétaires-viticulteurs*, who also have some of the best sites and some of the lowest yields per hectare. *Propriétaires-viticulteurs* account for about 25 per cent to 30 per cent of the production, but a much smaller percentage of the exports.

HOW TO READ AN ALSACE LABEL

All Alsace wines must have the following information on the label: Produce of France, the bottle size (at present 70cl or 75cl, but soon to be just 75cl), the name of the producer and the words Appellation Alsace Contrôlée. In addition, they may add the name of a *lieu-dit* (a vineyard or site name), they may add a cuvée name, e.g. *Les Écaillers*, and they may add other optional information, i.e. 'dry white wine', 'serve chilled'. In the case of a Grand Cru, the words Appellation Alsace Grand Cru Contrôlée, the vintage and the grape variety must appear, together with the name of the vineyard. In the case of a Vendange Tardive, the vintage and grape variety must appear.

Grand Cru wine (optional, as this is mentioned at the foot of the label as well)
Vintage (compulsory, as the wine is Grand Cru)
Domaine *name (optional, as the* vigneron*'s name is mentioned below)*
'Late Picked' (see Appellation Contrôlée laws)

Grape variety (compulsory)
Vineyard site (compulsory)
Appellation Grand Cru Contrôlée (compulsory)
Domaine *bottled (not always the case with some producers, who may have the wine bottled for them)*
Vigneron*'s name (either this or the estate name are compulsory)*
Address (compulsory)
Produce of France (compulsory)
Size (compulsory)

Facing page
Appellation Contrôlée (compulsory)
Producer's name (compulsory, but also mentioned below)
Variety (optional, as not Grand Cru or Vendange Tardive)
Cuvée name (optional)
Vintage (optional, as not Grand Cru or Vendange Tradive)
Size (compulsory)
Produce of France (compulsory)
Name and address (compulsory)

ADDITIONAL STRIP LABELLING

In addition to a body label, and usually a neck label, Alsace producers seem inordinately fond of adding another label between the two, usually to show that a medal has been attained, occasionally to show a cuvée name, and sometimes to give extra information, e.g. Vendange Tardive. Sometimes the cuvée label will be almost indistinguishable from a medal label in shape and colouring, without close inspection. Here are a few labels that might be seen.

COLMAR

Wine Fair Medals
The most frequently seen are medals for wine fairs. Of these the fair at Colmar is probably the most popular. It is to some extent a guarantee of quality, and many consumers buy on this basis in France – the wine fairs issue a book of 'winners', with the name, address and cuvée which won a prize. But it is a poor wine indeed that cannot win a prize in some of the shows, and many of the top producers never enter their wines, so that medal winners should not be followed too slavishly.

CONFRÉRIE SAINT-ÉTIENNE

Confrérie St-Étienne
Tastings for the sigille are carried out each year (see page 250). This seal is quite highly prized, but again, many producers do not enter their wines, and only a small proportion of the total wines produced are judged.

CUVÉE VIEILLES VIGNES

'Old Vines'. No legal definition, and old vines can be of whatever age the producer wishes. It could be a very good product, but must be taken in conjunction with the reputation of the grower.

SÉLECTION DE GRAINS NOBLES

'picked grape by grape, affected by noble rot', if this is stated it should be true . . . Often numbered bottles for late-picked wines, which enhances their value.

VITICULTURE

Viticulture, the art of growing the vines to produce the fruit which will eventually be turned into wine, is increasingly taking on the aspect of a science. Until the end of the last century, growers continued to look after their vines in the traditional ways handed down from generation to generation. Before phylloxera, vines were propagated by layering (pegging a branch below ground level, where it would sprout roots, and eventually become an independent plant). If the branch were held under ground level for the whole of its length, several plants could be propagated in this way, and the vineyard quickly and cheaply replenished. For this reason, vineyards were not generally planted in the neat rows which we see today. The vines were trained *en quenouille*: each vine, or group of up to three vines, was trained up a stout oak or chestnut stake, about three metres in height. The main trunks were trained up to a height of 60 centimetres to one metre, and then spur-pruned, with one long cane left on each, about a metre in length, curled back onto the main stem and tied 20 centimetres from the ground. The new growth from the crown of the vine was allowed to grow to the top of the pole, for use as next year's replacement wood, and the new growth from further down the cane was trimmed in June and August, allowing sufficient growth to ripen the crop of fruit, but preventing the vigour of the vine from use in vegetation rather than fruit production. For traditional reasons it was usual to plant three vines in each hole, although it was discovered at the end of the nineteenth century that the vines were healthier and more vigorous, producing a larger crop per vine, when planted singly. The growers around this time planted the vines singly, with three main trunks per vine. The density of plantation was quite high, with vines spaced at between 80cm and 1·3m apart. At the extreme north of the region, at Wissembourg, the vines were trained on a high trellis, about one metre above ground level, known as a *Kammerbau*.

Guyot, the eminent viticulturist, wrote in 1876 that the average yield in Alsace was some 50 hectolitres per hectare, which was high compared with other regions of France. He also wrote that on occasions some of the more fertile vineyards of Alsace had been known to produce yields as high as 150 to 200 hectolitres per hectare!

At this time, most vineyards were planted with a mixture of vines, although some villages and vineyards had a particular reputation for one variety, such as Ottrott for Pinot Noir, Riquewihr for Muscat, and Wolxheim for Riesling.

With the advent of oidium, a virulent fungal disease brought in on vines from America, followed by phylloxera, an aphid which reached Europe by the same means and completely destroyed vines by burrowing its way into the roots and leaves, many vineyards were devastated by the early 1900s. Yields were reduced to between six and eight hectolitres per hectare and many growers faced penury. It became much more expensive to maintain a vineyard against diseases. The Germans forbade grafting onto phylloxera-resistant rootstocks, although this was producing good results in Bordeaux and Burgundy, and instructed the growers to use chemical fumigators on the vineyards instead. The vineyard owners were still arguing this point in 1914, when war broke out. Chrétien Oberlin, a research viticulturist, made numerous attempts to cross and clone vines to give good quality at the same time as disease resistance, and together with some of the major proprietors of the region, achieved some useful progress. The viticultural research station, which had started in a small way in Rouffach in 1874, was enlarged and moved to Colmar in 1895, and Chrétien Oberlin donated his collection of around 500 vine varieties. He was the technical director of the research institute until his death in 1915.

During the war, the vineyards naturally suffered from neglect, and a series of humid summers aggravated the problems, leaving the vineyards in a very poor condition in 1918, ravaged by cryptogamic diseases, phylloxera and other insect pests. The only vines comparatively unaffected were some of Oberlin's hybrid vines, such as the red Oberlin 595. The argument continued, debating whether the vineyards should be replanted with noble varieties or with disease resistant hybrids. The 1921 vintage proved a turning point for the better growers, the traditional noble varieties producing a truly wonderful wine, whilst the hybrids were unable to produce more than mediocre quality. The vines from the hybrid wines were unable to compete in quality with the cheap wines of other regions. In 1925 an Association des Viticulteurs was formed, to promote replanting with noble varieties, and by 1948 the area under vine had been reduced to 9,500 hectares (from 25,000 hectares in 1903), with the hybrid vines planted in the poorly placed areas being suppressed.

Nowadays, the vines are generally trained to a height of 60 to 90 centimetres above the soil, with either one or two canes curved over wires in an arc formation, carrying between eight and fifteen buds per vine. (The AC allows 12 buds per square metre.) Vines are generally grown at a distance of 1·4 to 1·5 square metres, giving a density of 4,400 to 4,800 vines per hectare, although there are large differences between spacing and pruning in individual vineyards, some growers believing that a greater density of vines leads to a more concentrated wine, each vine producing less and therefore concentrating the elements available from the soil. Height also can make a great difference; vines trained closer to the soil can benefit from greater heat reflection, although they are more prone to frost damage, unless the site is steeply sloping. Occasionally vines may be spur-pruned, the permanent trunk of the vine extending in an inverted L shape, the new shoots each year coming from buds left on the arm of the trunk. Where tractors are used within the vineyard, distances between rows will be adapted to accommodate their passage, sometimes alternating a wide row with two or three narrower rows.

All vines are now grafted onto phylloxera-resistant rootstocks and these also can make a great difference to the quality of the wine produced. Rootstocks not only save the wine from the attacks of phylloxera, but also control the vigour of the vine, affect the growth pattern through the year and the intake of vital elements from the soil. Research into the possibilities of different rootstocks is still in progress, but it has been shown that given identical soil, climate, and vine variety, differences between rootstocks can produce a marked difference in the vine's behaviour and in the final constituents of the grapes produced. Many of Alsace's vineyards are planted on vigorous rootstocks, which cause the vine to produce foliage at the expense of fruit – according to one eminent winemaker, 70 per cent of Alsace is on the wrong rootstocks at present! Less vigorous rootstocks give vines with less luxuriant foliage, but with grapes capable of higher sugar and mineral concentration. However, young vines can take up to five years to produce their first crop, compared with only three years with a more vigorous rootstock.

The vinegrower's work consists of pruning and tying up the canes in the spring, before budding commences around April. Weed control must be carried out, either by chemical or mechanical means. Many growers sow a ground crop for cover, which is ploughed into the soil to give nitrogen. Others leave a ground crop permanently in place, preventing erosion on the slopes, providing some fertilisation and forcing the vine roots to search deeper into the soil for nutrients. Throughout the growing season a watch must be kept for signs of mildew or disease, and the vineyard will be sprayed between four and seven times a year, depending on the rainfall, the temperature and the presence of any infection. After flowering is complete, when the grower can see the size of the potential crop, he may decide to remove some of the clusters to reduce the crop and gain intensity in the remaining bunches. This may also be carried out through the summer, removing either damaged or excess grapes and concentrating the vine's energy on the remaining bunches. The foliage must also be controlled, tied up where necessary and pruned to provide sufficient foliage to ripen the grapes, but not excessive foliage which would divert the vine's energy. In the autumn, the grower must monitor the rising sugar levels and ripeness of the grapes, to decide the optimum moment for picking, once the picking date has been set for the year.

In all, Sittler estimates, in *Terroirs et Vins d'Alsace*, that the grower will work for an average of 410 hours per hectare per year without mechanisation, with an additional 310 hours per hectare for the vintage. A more steeply sloping vineyard will obviously take more man-hours than a flatter area and a more painstaking grower will spend more time monitoring and regulating the size of his crop than a grower who is simply looking for volume.

The vintage can take up to five or six weeks, as the different varieties ripen at different speeds, and the grower will also decide whether to take the gamble of leaving his grapes longer on the vines for a greater maturity or a Vendange Tardive.

VINIFICATION

After picking, the grapes are taken to the press-house. The grapes may be picked over to remove any damaged or rotten bunches, or these may have been eliminated at the time of picking if this has been done by hand. The grapes may be broken up in a type of 'mincer' or *fouloir*, to facilitate pressing, and they may be wholly or partially de-stemmed for the Pinot Noir, to eliminate the bitter taste that stems could impart to the wine during maceration. Grapes may also be placed into the presses without any breaking up, which helps to prevent oxidation.

The sugar content is measured at picking time to estimate the potential alcohol: the more sugar in the grapes, the higher the alcohol content in the finished wine. Sugar content is measured in degrees oechsle, as in Germany. This is a measure of the specific gravity and the potential alcohol can be found by dividing the figure given by eight.

Traditionally, grapes were pressed in wooden presses, the solid wood base descending onto the cake of grapes by turning a central screw. The pressure exerted was even and gentle, and the juice extracted was clear – mud and other elements having been strained by the passage of the juice through the mass of skins and stalks. When the pressure did not extract any more juice, the wooden base would be lifted and the cake broken up and re-pressed. This method was cumbersome, time-consuming and labour-intensive. The wooden presses took up a lot of valuable space, had to be filled and emptied by hand, and have now largely been superseded by mechanical presses. The most commonly found, the Vaslin, is a cylindrical horizontal steel tube, fitted with plates at either end, with chains attached in the middle. The grapes are put inside, the plates squash them towards the centre, whilst the chains break up the cake of stems and skins to facilitate extraction of the juice. These presses take between 300 kilos and 40,000 kilos of grapes at a time. They can be set to different speeds of pressing and different intensities of juice extraction. The juice is not as clear as that from the old wooden presses and must be allowed to settle in order to remove any impurities. The speed of pressing has an important effect on the quality of the juice, slower pressing giving a more gentle extraction. This can be a problem for the co-operatives and for *négociants*, when grapes might be arriving at the press-houses in quick succession.

Many winemakers are now turning from the Vaslin to the more expensive pneumatic press, also a steel cylinder, but with an inflatable bag inside, which squashes the grapes against the side of the cylinder as it inflates. This is much more gentle and gives a much cleaner juice. The speed and intensity of pressing can be set, as with the Vaslin, and there is more flexibility as to the weight of grapes per pressing. The main makes of bladder press are the Bucher, from the same manufacturers as the Vaslin, and the Willmes. These presses cost about twice as much as a Vaslin.

After pressing, the juice is allowed to settle if necessary, to remove impurities, or centrifuged to clear the juice more quickly. Any necessary adjustments are made, for protein stability, acidity, or chaptalisation (the addition of sugar). Sometimes a yeast culture is added, especially in a wet year, where the natural yeasts may be less plentiful, but usually the natural yeasts present on the grapeskins are preferred. A small amount of sulphur dioxide is added to remove any bacteria and to allow the yeast to get under way. The juice is pumped into a fermentation vat, which may be of wood, stainless steel or concrete, and fermentation starts.

The cellars are usually cold at this period of the year and the traditional thick wooden vats give good temperature insulation, but increasingly winemakers are installing systems of temperature control, often by ingeniously adapting the old traditional wooden vats with a system of piping which passes cold water through the vats. The temperature of fermentation will depend on the grape variety and on the style of wine being produced. Generally a lower temperature of around 14–16°C will be used for a lighter, more floral wine, such as a Sylvaner or a Muscat, and a higher temperature of up to 20–21°C will be used for a heavier, more spicy varietal such as Gewurztraminer. It has been shown that temperature control can greatly affect the bouquet and structure of a wine and also its ageing potential. Temperature control also helps the winemaker to keep to an ideal curve of sugar/alcohol conversion and gives greater control over the speed and progress of fermentation.

When fermentation is complete, the wine is racked off the deposit, or lees, into a clean container, either of wood or of steel. Generally speaking, the malolactic fermentation, the bacterial conversion of malic acid into the softer lactic acid, is not desired in white Alsace wines, and care will be taken to avoid this by keeping the wine cool, adjusting the sulphur content if necessary and by keeping the cellar scrupulously clean. Sometimes the wine is fined with bentonite, or centri-fuged, to clarify it, or it may be left to fall bright in the cool cellar. Occasionally winemakers allow the malolactic fer-mentation to take place, occasionally they are unable to prevent it, when it follows hard on the alcoholic fermentation. It generally leads to the wine being softer, rounder and a little more 'buttery' in flavour, with a less floral bouquet. It is less important with Gewurztraminer or Tokay, but can impair the flavour of Riesling or Muscat. Some growers are ex-perimenting with the ageing of whites in new oak *barriques*, and in this case the malolactic will take place, as it is very hard to prevent, and also the character of the wine will be more in keeping with a fatter, rounder style of wine.

The wine will usually be filtered and bottled before the summer following the vintage, the better wines being kept in cask a little longer and bottled in the autumn. Each grower has to obtain a Certificat d'Agrément before bottling and commer-cialising his wine. This will detail the quantities produced of each varietal and the wines will be tasted blind by a committee to assess their typicity.

Pinot Noir undergoes a slightly different vinification: the colour is to be extracted from the grape skins, so unlike the white varieties the juice cannot immediately be separated from the skins. Traditionally, the grapes are broken up and the juice macerated with the skins. This is the cheapest method. Often a small percentage of fermenting juice will be added to the vat to start the fermentation and to improve colour extraction. Alter-natively, the juice and skins can be heated, the warm juice macerated a few hours, then pressed and vinified as for a white wine. The third method of production is by *macération carbon-ique*, the enclosed carbonic maceration of the whole uncrushed grapes, the traditional method in the Beaujolais region and in much of the south of France. This produces a wine which has good colour, is very fruity when young, but does not age well. It is often used in combination with one of the first two methods, a part of the juice being separately vinified and the two vats blended after fermentation.

Pinot Noir always undergoes malolactic fermentation, which is necessary for a red wine, giving stability as well as a more complete flavour. In recent years Pinot Noir is often aged in small *barriques*, to give a more oaky flavour, although traditionally the reds, as with the white wines of the region, are vinified and matured in large old oak casks, which were not meant to impart any wood flavour to the wine. Experiments are taking place with the local Vosges oak, as well as barrels made from Limousin, to produce a more powerful, richly-coloured red wine. The colour of the Pinot Noir varies from light rosé to quite a respectable deeper red, depending on the method and length of colour extraction. As with the whites, it is usually bottled in the spring or autumn following the vintage.

Late-picked wines, the Vendange Tardive and Sélection de Grains Nobles, follow the same general rules of winemaking, the fermentation generally taking place at a low temperature because the grapes are picked late into the year, often in November or December. The greater concentration of sugar and the low temperature combine to give a long slow fermentation. The final alcohol content for these wines can vary greatly, from 12·5° to over 15°, and the fermentation may be allowed to take its course or may be stopped to retain a greater degree of sweetness in the finished wine.

SOILS

The soil texture is very important to the quality of wine produced. Firstly, a soil with good drainage is essential to any vine. The roots of a mature vine extend deep into the soil, and whilst they must find sufficient moisture to live, they do not like to be permanently waterlogged. Different soil textures will have different water-retaining potential, and the porosity or compactness of the soil will also effect the development pattern of the vine's roots and the depth and quantities at which side roots are formed, thus affecting the mineral intake of the vine. A vine will produce grapes from its third year, but requires at least eight years to form a full root structure, and will continue to develop its structure and to produce better wines until it reaches an optimum at the age of around 20 to 30 years old. Poor vintages are less of a problem for mature vines than for young vines: frost is less likely to cause permanent damage to deep-rooted vines, in a heavy downfall it is the surface roots that will suck in the largest volume of water fastest, causing grapes to become waterlogged and sometimes to split. Also, in a dry vintage, the deeper root structure is less affected, as it can still find sufficient water far below the surface area.

The soil is also the essential source of mineral elements in the grape and these nutrients are partly retained in the wine. Salts of major elements such as calcium, potassium and magnesium, and trace elements such as iron, zinc and manganese help in the development of the vine and in the production of the wine.

The Alsace soil pattern is extremely varied. During the formation of the Vosges mountains various soil types were thrown together haphazardly, and one can find soils derived from rocks of totally differing eras and formations nestling side by side along the length of the Vosges foothills. There are some 20 major soil formations in Alsace, each having some bearing upon the character of the wine produced. Nearer the Vosges mountains, the more steeply-sloping vineyards, often terraced, have a thin topsoil, with subsoils of weathered granite, gneiss, sandstone, schist and various volcanic sediments. On the gentler slopes there are subsoils of clay and marl or weathered limestone and sandstone in varying proportions, under a deeper layer of topsoil. As the hills flatten onto the plain, the soils are generally alluvial deposits, with various soil components eroded from the mountains and with a deeper, more fertile topsoil. The fertility of this last favours large yields, with a corresponding lack of individuality and of quality.

Generally speaking, a heavy clay or marl soil suits Gewurz-traminer and Tokay-Pinot Gris, helping to give body and weight and more rapid evolution, whereas limestone gives lighter weight, more perfumed wine, often with less complexity. Granite soil gives elegance and finesse, and rock, such as flint, slate and schist also has a particular individual character, almost 'gunflint', well suited to Riesling.

A lighter textured soil is also warmer, drying out more rapidly after rain than a heavy textured clay soil. This affects the speed of ripening of the grapes, as does the angle and aspect of a slope, presenting the sun's rays at a better angle to the vine and reflecting heat, whilst sheltering the vineyard from winds. The early-ripening varieties, such as Chasselas, Pinot Gris and Muscat Ottonel, are more adaptable in their choice of soils, whereas the later-ripening varieties, such as Riesling, Muscat D'Alsace and Sylvaner, need a warmer soil.

All these factors, which may at first seem rather irrelevant and remote from the wine in the glass, do have a very strong direct bearing on the taste.

The yield must also be considered. If the yield is very high, every constituent of the juice will be diluted further and the wine will have less individual character. The smaller the yield, the more concentrated the juice will be and the more likely the wine will be to exhibit strong individuality of character.

The whole essence of soil structure, position, aspect and microclimate is summarised by the French term *terroir*.

VARIETAL LABELLING

A varietal wine is simply one that is named after a grape variety. Nearly all Alsace wines are varietal wines, although until this century most Alsace wines were made from a blend of varieties, the only distinction being between 'noble' blends and everyday blends.

Most producers grow a range of varieties, even if they have only very small holdings of land. Many growers have parcels of land on different types of soil, with different microclimates, and the range of varietals means the most suitable grape can be matched to the soil. Picking is spread over a period of six weeks and each varietal is vinified separately. Much of the wine is sold at the cellar door and the producer is able to sell a range of wines, at a range of prices to suit the individual customer. Some varietals will be cheaper to produce, giving larger yields and being less temperamental.

In addition, many winemakers will make more than one cuvée of the better grape varieties each year: maybe from riper grapes, or younger vines, maybe from different vineyard sites, maybe a Vendange Tardive or Sélection de Grains Nobles (or both), maybe simply different styles to suit different purposes. As many of these are labelled 'Réserve', 'Special Réserve', 'Réserve Personelle' 'Sélection Personelle', 'Cuvée Exceptionelle', or 'Cuvée . . .', none of which have any legal meaning, it is often confusing for the customer. Under each varietal, therefore, I have listed the cuvées available from each producer, with an indication of the style, price range and quality of each.

A detailed description of the style of each variety heads each chapter.

RIESLING

The Riesling grape variety originated in Germany, in the Rhine valley. It was first introduced into France in the Loire valley, and was known as the *gentil aromatique*. It was later abandoned in this area as the soil and climate were not particularly suitable. The earliest mention of the Riesling in Alsace seems to be in 1477, under the name Rissling, but it is hard to be precise, as the variety had several names at this time. *Gentil* meant 'discreet', and Alsace vine sales catalogues of the nineteenth century list various vines 'red *gentil*', 'green *gentil*', etc. Cyrus Redding states in 1833: 'The white Gentil reaches perfection in ten years, and will keep good a hundred'. In 1875, Vizitelly comments, in his *Wines of the World*, of Alsace wines, that 'their principal merit is that in spite of their ordinary indifferent quality they will keep for at least a generation. Certain of them made from the Riesling grape will carry their thirty years as though they were merely three, retaining moreover their strong gunflint flavour as in their most juvenile days.' He names the best wines as the Hunneweyers and Osterbergers, both regions still well known for their Rieslings. Guyot, in his *Étude des Vignobles de France*, in 1876, states that the Rieslings in the Bas Rhin are remarkable for their flavour, force and longevity, which has practically no limits.

The Riesling has always been considered one of the highest quality grape varieties for the region, but has only been planted on a wide scale in Alsace during the twentieth century, after the First World War, and it is still increasing its percentage of the vineyard area.

It is a late-ripening grape, producing its best wines where it has had a slow, cool, lengthy, ripening period, and it has the advantage that it will continue to ripen even in cool, late-autumn weather, when the temperatures are too low for many other varieties. It prefers a schist or granite soil and needs a well-sheltered site, as picking will often be as late as November.

Riesling generally has a very distinct, steely acidity, with lightly aromatic fruit and often a grassiness when young. The flavour lasts well in the mouth and the wine should have great elegance and breeding. The best wines will be very firm, with a clean, positive flavour that develops as the wine gets older. The alcohol level is generally only moderate, between 10 and 12 degrees. With ageing, the wines often take on a slightly 'petrolly', flinty nose and taste and ripe vintages will develop a warm peachiness. Even Vendange Tardive wines are usually bone-dry. Good Riesling can have great austerity when young, with sometimes a green appley nose and palate. It is probably one of the hardest varieties to appreciate when immature, although it is the one that will provide the most quality potential when old.

A simple Riesling usually needs to be kept for two to four years from the vintage, a Réserve wine four to eight years, and a good Grand Cru or top cuvée often needs a minimum of six to ten years before it will show at its best. A top wine from a good vintage will keep happily for 20 to 40 years, developing a more intense floral complex bouquet, and an almost 'oily', steely, aggressively positive flavour in the mouth. This is the longest-lived of all Alsace wines.

The problem with Riesling is that it is very difficult to appreciate when too young: unlike most Alsace varietals, it will often have little or no bouquet, and taste rather acidic and unyielding. The wines available to the customer are often too young, as neither the growers nor the wine merchants can afford to hang on to these wines for a sufficient length of time. The customer knows that he has to lay down Clarets and Burgundies, but is used to buying other wines as required, ready to drink. For this reason, Riesling is less popular than it deserves to be. It is not an easy grape to understand and the consumer needs to work at it. Also, the word 'Riesling' is extremely over-worked, and it is hard for the consumer to distinguish on the shelf between German Riesling, Yugoslav Laski Riesling, Italian Riesling Italico, Californian Emerald Riesling and all the other multitude of Riesling wines that exist. Often, too, there are cheap Alsace Rieslings that lack the characteristics described above, being produced in vast quantities in high-yielding areas and sold for the lowest possible prices. At best, these are bland, unexciting wines, and at worst, thin and acidic.

Alsace Riesling can be served as an aperitif or with shellfish and fish dishes. Its clean acidity goes well with *choucroute garnie* or with white meat dishes. The peachier, softer riper styles could be served with pâtés or with foie gras, although personally I prefer the somewhat fuller weightier style of Tokay-Pinot Gris with foie gras.

There are around 2,700 hectares of Riesling in Alsace and plantations are increasing in place of other varietals such as Sylvaner. Riesling must attain a minimum potential alcohol of 8·5° before chaptalisation, with a maximum of 13°. For the wine to be labelled Grand Cru, it must attain a minimum of 10° (170 gms/lit sugar) before enrichment, with a maximum of 13·5°. For Grand Cru, the yield is lowered from 100 hectolitres per hectare to a maximum of 70 hectolitres per hectare. Riesling can be Vendange Tardive or Sélection de Grains Nobles, although in practice the latter is rarely attained. Vendange Tardive must attain a minimum potential alcohol of 12·9° (220 gms/lit sugar), and Sélection de Grains Nobles a minimum of 15·1° potential alcohol (256 gms/lit sugar). Neither of these categories can be enriched in any way.

RIESLING

JEAN-BAPTISTE ADAM, Ammerschwihr
Négociant
Kaefferkopf (1983/85)   2 ★
> Develops rich, spicy, ripe fruit nose after 4 to 5 years. Quite broad, floral, spicy fruit on palate, soft, ripe, quite powerful. Rich, quite soft style. Medium term keeping. 5-8 years.

Generic (1985)   1
> A little lightweight, dilute, soft. Pleasant, light, floral fruit, without much varietal flavour and a little short on finish.

Letzenberg (1985)   2
> Lighter fruit than the Kaefferkopf, more herbaceous, sappy. Clean, fresh, youthful fruit, lean, herbal character. Attractive lightweight style. Medium term keeping. 5-8 years.

See also Vendange Tardive

DOMAINE LUCIEN ALBRECHT, Orschwihr
Propriétaire viticulteur
Clos Himmelreich   2
> Clean, light, floral fruit, elegant, dry, with medium weight. Attractive, sappy fruit, with good balancing acidity. Medium term keeping. 5-8 years.

Cuvée Henri Albrecht ③

More weighty, earthy, powerful fruit. More solid structure, minerally, with good keeping properties. 6-10 years.

Grand Cru Pfingstberg (1983/85) ③ ★/★★

Very distinctive minerally nose, which takes time to develop. Fresh clean fruit on the palate, steely, minerally, much less forward. Very good length of flavour, which takes time to develop. Long term keeping.

See also Vendange Tardive

VICTOR ANCEL, Kayserberg

Propriétaire viticulteur

Grand Cru Schlossberg (1985) ② ★

Develops petrolly, minerally nose after 2 to 3 years. Rich, ripe, broad fruit on palate, floral, with soft acidity. Big, broad style, which develops oily, earthy, petrol aromas quite early on. Medium term keeping. 4-8 years.

CAVE CO-OPÉRATIVE D'ANDLAU, Barr

Co-operative

Grand Cru Wiebelsberg, Réserve du Président (1985) ②

Soft, herbal, fruit nose. Soft, ripe, herbaceous fruit on the palate, marred by slight sulphur. Quite evolved, earthy style, broader, less elegant. A little disappointing for a Grand Cru. Keep 4-6 years.

Divinal (nv) ①

Clean, fresh, light, floral on nose and palate, very pleasant, without any great depth of flavour. Medium length, with some varietal character. Good 'supermarket' Riesling.

CAVE VINICOLE DE BEBLENHEIM – see BARON DE HOEN

GASTON BECK, Zellenberg
Négociant
1985 ☑

Soft, round, gently floral style, with softer, less marked acidity. Quite forward wine, not for long keeping. 2-3 years. A little short on the finish, but pleasant.

J. BECKER (same firm as above), Zellenberg
Négociant
1985 ☑

Similar to the above wine, but I found this example a little flat and dull, with less varietal character.

CAVE CO-OPÉRATIVE DE BENNWIHR & ENVIRONS, Bennwihr
Co-operative
1985/83 ☐ / ☑

Soft, floral, broad, almost buttery Riesling, with good varietal character. Gentle fruit, evolving quite rapidly, with light acidity. Pleasant, lightweight, with quite good varietal flavour, not for long keeping. 2-4 years.

LÉON BEYER, Eguisheim
Négociant
Generic (1983/85/86) ☐ / ☑ ★

Clean, crisp, young wine, fresh, flowery, with steely, slightly spicy fruit, and more character than most generic wines of its price. Quite lightweight, delicate, but with good acidity, and clean dry varietal flavour. Well-made, medium ageing potential. 3-6 years.

Réserve (1983/85) ☑

Selected from above, with higher oechsle, and therefore a little more weight of fruit. Same steely, clean-cut, elegant, dry style, very much a wine for food. Good varietal character, very classy. 5-6 years. Even older vintages, such as 1960 tasted recently, retain lovely purity of flavour.

Les Écaillers (1983/84/85) ☑ ★★

A crisp, dry style, made to accompany shellfish. From Beyer's own vineyards, partly from Pfersigberg. Floral, lemony acidity, with good backbone, and long powerful steely flavour. Develops good petrolly character with age. Not made in every vintage. Good keeping ability, keep 5-8 years.

Cuvée Particulière (1967/71/76/83) ③ ★★★

Picked late in the season, between 90 and 100 oechsle. Only produced in the best vintages. Big boned, steely, flinty, floral Riesling, with intense steely power. Big, broad, intense, with good balancing acidity. Lovely petrol character develops with age. For long keeping, 8-10 years minimum.

PAUL BLANCK, DOMAINE DES COMTES DE LUPFEN, Kientzheim

Propriétaire viticulteur (also *négociant* under name of Blanck Frères)

Réserve Spéciale (1985/87) ②

Grown on sandy soil near Ammerschwihr. Soft, young, sappy, floral fruit, lean, dry, with medium weight and length. Light, pleasant varietal flavour, without any great character.

Patergarten (1987) ②

Broader, softer fruit, more solid. Less racy. Quite herbal Riesling, with medium length. Clean, well balanced, medium weight. Gentle, soft style, for medium term keeping. 4-6 years.

Furstentum (1983/81/85/86/87) ② / ③

A separate cuvée is made from young and old vines. (The

APPELLATION ALSACE CONTROLEE

Riesling Furstentum

Mise en Bouteilles au Domaine

BLANCK

Domaine des Comtes de Lupfen

Domaine des Comtes de Lupfen. Propriété de Paul Blanck et ses fils à Kientzheim (Kaysersberg) Haut-Rhin - France.

Vieilles Vignes is from vines of 20 years and older.) Quite sappy, herbal, spicy, rich riesling fruit, broad, soft, ripe, with an almost buttery, creamy fruit. Develops petrol/oiliness after 5 to 8 years, but then starts to fade. Keep 3-6 years.

EMILE BOECKEL, Mittelbergheim
Négociant
Brandluft (1985)   ② / ③
Light, fresh, floral Riesling, without great weight. Soft acidity, fresh, quite clean, but a little lightweight. Pleasant. For medium term keeping. 5-7 years.
Zotzenberg (1985)   ②
Perfumed, floral, aromatic nose and palate, gentle, sappy, soft young fruit, very clean, with medium weight. Fresh, lightweight, herbal attractive style, without much length. Medium term keeping. 5-7 years.
Grand Cru Wiebelsberg (1985)   ② / ③
Lighter, more lemony fresh fruit, crisp, youthful sappy Riesling, with clean, smoky, floral fruit on the palate. A little more intensity of flavour, with lightweight but well-balanced riesling character. Medium term keeping. 5-8 years.

BOTT FRÈRES, Ribeauvillé
Propriétaire viticulteur
Réserve (1986)   ① / ②
Light, soft, floral riesling fruit, medium length and weight. Quite gentle style, with soft balancing acidity, for drinking quite young.

3-6 years. The 1981 tasted recently had developed an attractive soft mature petrolly riesling flavour.

Réserve Exceptionelle (1986/85)   ② ★

Softer, more fruity style, with richer, fatter fruit on palate, and soft balancing acidity. Some residual sugar gives a broader, more floral/spicy style. Attractive, elegant riesling flavour, for medium term keeping. 4-8 years.

Réserve Personelle (1983/85)   ★②

The top cuvée, made from the free-run juice. Clean, floral, smoky, young fruit, crisp, attractive, fresh, with a little residual sugar. Quite rich, smoky, spicy riesling fruit, with good length of flavour. Develops soft, petrolly riesling character with age. Keep 5-8 years.

ALBERT BOXLER, Niedermorschwihr
Propriétaire viticulteur

Generic (1984/85)   ①

This wine is light, fresh, herbal, with an almost hessian, vegetal nose. Very fresh, lightweight, dry, with soft acidity. Attractive, gentle, lightweight wine for medium term keeping. 3-6 years.

Grand Cru Sommerberg (1983/85)   ②

Soft, gentle spicy, smoky, ripe fruit, quite broad, floral, and rich in style. Gentle, floral style, quite perfumed, smoky, with light balancing acidity. Not heavy, but well-balanced, delicate style with surprisingly good keeping ability. 4-8 years.

Grand Cru Brand (1983/85)   ② ★

Light, steely, sappy, firm, dry riesling fruit, with more backbone, and needing longer to come round. Lightly spicy, elegant, with more finesse, more acidity. Firmer wine, still quite delicate, but with more weight. Long term keeping. 5-10 years.

F. BRUCKER (formerly A. Gaschy), Wettolsheim
Négociant

Cuvée Tradition (1985)   ①

Spicy nose, almost Tokay-like. Quite high acidity on palate, with herbal, buttery fruit, slightly almondy, and a little mean, unripe. Not very Riesling in character. Not recommended.

DOMAINE MARCEL DEISS (Jean-Michel Deiss), Bergheim,
Propriétaire viticulteur

A multitude of labels here, with eight basic cuvées each year, and late-picked wines in top vintages.

Bennwihr (1986)   ② ★

Light, floral nose, which evolves quickly. Clean, slightly appley, young riesling fruit, fresh, lightweight, with good length of flavour. Soft, ripe, gentle fruit, for medium term keeping. 2-6 years.

St Hippolyte (1986/85) ☑
Clean, fresh, floral riesling nose. Quite positive acidity on the palate, with a hint of sulphur. Floral, medium weight, with rich, ripe fruit balancing acidity, and quite a lemony, herbal character. Unknit when young, needs time to come together. Medium term keeping. 5-8 years.

Bergheim, Engelgarten (1985/86) ☑
Light, minerally, floral nose. Youthful, confectionery fruit on the palate, with good acidity, and quite lemony fruit. Herbal, lean fruit, which takes time to evolve. Medium length. Medium to long term keeping. 6–10 years.

Bergheim, Grasberg (1985/86) ☑
Light, herbal, lemony riesling fruit, with a good varietal character. Fresh youthful fruit, minerally, lemony, with quite high acidity. Fresh, clean, young fruit, with more weight and character. Needs time to evolve. Medium to long term keeping. 6-10 years.

Bergheim, Burg (1985/86) ☑
Develops quite petrolly spicy nose, with a more solid, earthy, sturdy style on the palate. Still good balancing acidity, with more

weighty fruit, and more feeling of alcohol. Powerful wine, for medium-long term keeping. 6-10 years.

Grand Cru Altenberg de Bergheim (1982/83/85) ③ ★

Develops quite petrolly riesling nose after 4-5 years. Full bodied, dry but with rich fruit, powerful, sometimes a little clumsy and heavyweight, but with very good length of ripe riesling flavour. Strongly varietal, spicy, with good length. Long term keeping. 5-10+ years.

Grand Cru Schoenenberg (1985) ③ ★

Hints of petrolly, ripe Riesling on the nose after three years. Clean, ripe riesling fruit, with soft spiciness, and light balancing acidity. Medium weight, less concentrated than expected from the nose. Still unknit, needs time to evolve. Well-made wine with good varietal flavour.

See also Vendange Tardive

JEAN PIERRE DIRLER, Bergholtz

Propriétaire viticulteur

Grand Cru Kessler (1984/85) ② ★

Spicy, herbal, lemony riesling nose, which develops well in 3-4 years. Delicate fruit on the palate, clean, with a hint of lemon. Floral, aromatic, ripe fruit on the palate, never heavy, but with elegant lightness and delicate balance. Gently spicy, herbal and grapey, medium length. Medium term keeping. 4-8+ years.

Grand Cru Spiegel (1984/85) 2 ★

Clean, crisp riesling fruit, more steely, powerful. Firm lemony, flinty Riesling on palate, with good length and balance. Very well-made. For medium to long term keeping. 5-10+ years.

DOPFF AU MOULIN, Riquewihr

Négociant

1983/85 1 / 2

Soft, spicy, gentle fruit, with clean balancing acidity. The wines with the diamond shaped labels are from bought-in grapes, whilst the square-labelled wines are from their own vineyards and have much more weight and substance.

See also Vendange Tardive

DOPFF & IRION, Riquewihr

Négociant

Les Murailles (1985) 2

Light, fresh, herbal fruit. Slight spritz on the palate, with good weight of fruit, but rather hard, dull flavour. A little cardboardy, flat. Rather soft flavour, lacking in life. I have found this wine disappointing on several occasions.

See also Vendange Tardive

DOMAINE EHRHART, Ammerschwihr

Négociant

Generic (1985) 2

Soft, ripe, floral riesling nose, almost peachy. Ripe, soft, peachy fruit on the palate, quite spicy, attractive. Richer, fatter style, less varietal, with a little residual sugar. Medium length. Short term keeping. 3-5 years.

FÉLIX EPPELÉ, Ammerschwihr
Propriétaire viticulteur
Kaefferkopf (1985/86)　☒ ★
　Light, appley, young Riesling. Lightweight, crisp, clean, fresh, with appealing youthful fruit. Attractive, clean wine, without much depth, but with good balance.

FALLER, DOMAINE WEINBACH, Kayserberg/Kientzheim
Propriétaire viticulteur
Réserve Personelle (1983/85/82)   ☐2 ★

Very fragrant, floral nose, which develops a hint of petrol with 3 to 4 years. Very steely, clean, fragrant, and elegant, with lovely purity of riesling flavour. Classic style, which needs keeping 3-4 years, and will last much longer.

Grand Cru Schlossberg (1984/85)   ☐3 ★

Flowery, clean, rich riesling nose and palate, with more weight and power than the Réserve. Richer fruit, still very elegant, with a broader, more spicy fruit and needing a little longer. Long term keeping potential. Keep 5-10+ years.

Cuvée de la Sainte Catherine (1983/85/86)   ☐3 ★★

Intensely ripe, powerful, steely Riesling, with tremendous elegance. Powerful, appley richness when young, with very ripe, riesling fruit, and a very pure flavour. Slight residual sweetness/richness, with very good length of flavour. Very steely, well-structured fruit, needs at least 4-5 years, but will continue for many years. Picked around St Catherine's day, 25 November.

See also Vendange Tardive

LOUIS FREYBERGER, Bergheim
Propriétaire viticulteur
Grand Cru Altenberg de Bergheim (1983/85)   ☐2 ★

Very aromatic, smoky riesling nose, which takes 3-4 years to develop. Aromatic, ripe, powerful, petrolly flavour, with good riesling fruit, and broad spicy flavour. Good keeping potential. 6-10+ years.

VICTOR GAERTNER, Ammerschwihr
Propriétaire viticulteur
1985/86 ☑2

Clean, fresh, lightweight fruit, with good balancing acidity. Quite floral, soft, medium length, with good varietal flavour. For drinking quite young. 3-6 years.

Kaefferkopf (1985) ☑2

Floral nose. Clean, light, appley fruit on the palate, a little leaner in style, crisp, maybe a little sour on the finish. Fresh, pleasant, but not very exciting.

JÉROME GESCHICKT, Ammerschwihr
Propriétaire viticulteur
Kaefferkopf (1985/86) ☑2 ★

Very perfumed, floral, elderflower nose, unusual and distinctive. Fresh, aromatic, rich fruit on the palate, unusually broad, pungent, with clean ripe riesling fruit, and medium length. Medium term keeping, attractive when young. 3-5+ years.

ARMAND GILG, Mittelbergheim
Propriétaire viticulteur
Zotzenberg (1985) ☑2

Floral, herbal nose, a little sulphury. Rather hard, dull fruit on

the palate, with little riesling character, and a lack of ripeness.
Acceptable, but uninspiring.

Grand Cru Moenchberg (1985) ☑

Fresh, herbal, sappy nose. Quite high acidity on the palate, with
good fruit underlying. Good length of herbaceous riesling fruit,
which needs time to develop. Clean, quite steely, with good
varietal flavour. Keep 5-10+ years.

LOUIS GISSELBRECHT, Dambach-la-Ville
Négociant

Generic (1986/82) ☑ / ☑

Soft, attractive, light, floral nose. Lightweight, fresh, with soft,
ripe fruit, gentle, ripe style, medium length. Pleasant, with no
great individual character. For drinking young. 3-5 years.

WILLY GISSELBRECHT, Dambach-la-Ville
Négociant

Generic (1985) ☑ / ☑

Light, youthful, aromatic nose. Clean, attractive, light fruit on
the palate, not strongly marked, but well-balanced, fresh, quite
ripe. Good value for money. Pleasant wine for drinking quite
young. 3-5 years.

Réserve Spéciale (1986) ☑ / ☑

Fresh, lightweight, clean, with good varietal character. Quite
lean, floral style, light and dry, medium length, for drinking
young. 3-5 years.

Médaille d'Or (1985/86) ☑

More positive style, which develops petrolly flavour with 3-4

years. More weight of fruit, with lovely ripe riesling flavour, especially in the 1985. More solid, fleshy. Not for long keeping. 3-7 years.

ANDRÉ & REMY GRESSER, Andlau
Propriétaire viticulteur
Grand Cru Wiebelsberg (1984/85) ③ ★

Light, delicate, herbal style, dry, elegant and quite lean. Gentle lightweight fruit, fresh and well vinified even in the difficult 1984 vintage. Medium term keeping. 5-8+ years.

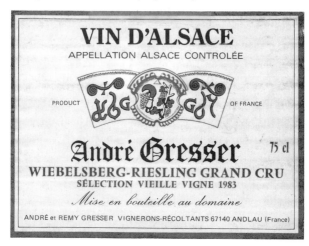

Grand Cru Wiebelsberg Vieilles Vignes (1983) ③ ★

Honeyed, grapefruit nose. Good weight of fruit on the palate, more powerful in style, dry and slightly hard. Less elegance, broader richer style of the vintage. Needs long keeping. 7-10+ years.

A. HELLMUTH, Dambach-la-Ville
Négociant
nv ①

Light, herbal riesling nose, with a hint of sulphur. Strong acidity on the palate, rather masking the light fruit. A little cardboardy/sulphury, without much riesling character. Not recommended.

E. HERING & FILS, Barr
Propriétaire viticulteur
Grand Cru Kirchberg de Barr (1983/84) ② ★

Floral, minerally nose, lightweight, very clean in the difficult 1984 vintage, richer but less clean in the more successful '83 vintage. Quite soft, gentle wine, disappointing in '83, but very attractive in '84.

JEAN HEYWANG, Heiligenstein
Propriétaire viticulteur
Generic (1985) ②

Soft, mild, gentle riesling fruit, never very aggressive, with light, mild acidity, and medium length. Very clean, but without great depth of flavour.

BARON DE HOEN, Beblenheim
Co-operative
Generic (1985)　②

Clean, floral, herbaceous riesling fruit, quite steely, well-balanced, with medium length. Spicy, cinnamon riesling flavour, with good potential for ageing. Well-made.

HUGEL & FILS, Riquewihr
Négociant
Generic (1983/84/85)　②

Clean, fresh and lightweight, with quite soft, broad, floral fruit in good vintages. Less successful in 1984. Medium length of clean, ripe fruit, without any great character. Keep for 3-5 years.

Cuvée Tradition (1985/86)　③

A little more weight than the generic, with a broader, fatter, richer fruit. Soft, forward, broad, fat style, with clean balancing acidity. Well-made, with medium length of flavour, but without great excitement. Reliable.

Réserve Personelle (1979/81/83/85)　③ ★/★★

Much more pungent, powerful style, with broad, earthy, rich riesling fruit, which develops a ripe petrolly/oily nose and palate after 5-6 years. Big, broad, heavy ripe style, almost with a hint of sweetness. Needs time to develop; keep for at least 6-8 years, and will last very much longer. Very well-made.

See also Vendange Tardive

MARCEL HUMBRECHT, Gueberschwihr
Propriétaire viticulteur
Cuvée Spéciale (1985)　②

Quite forward wine, with oily, petrolly nose developing after 2-3

years. Soft, quite fat style, a little blowsy. Ripe fruit, good varietal flavour, with rather soft acidity. For drinking fairly young. 3-6 years.

JOSMEYER, Wintzenheim
Négociant
Generic (1985) ① / ②
Quite forward wine, lean, fresh, with quite assertive acidity and ripe fruit to balance. Develops oily richness with 2-3 years, with soft, floral, ripe fruit. For drinking young. 2-5 years.

Les Pierrets (1983) ② ★
The better cuvée from Josmeyer has a rich, floral fruit and almost tropical fruit ripeness, with a little residual sugar and soft, fat richness of flavour. Medium term keeping. 5-8 years.

ANDRÉ KIENTZLER, Ribeauvillé
Propriétaire viticulteur
Osterberg (1983/85) ② ★
Ripe, smoky, spicy riesling fruit, very varietal, quite muscular style, which needs at least 4-5 years, and will last much longer. Steely, flinty structure, quite closed when young. Very well-made.
Grand Cru Geisberg (1982/83/85/86) ② / ③ ★★/★★★
Develops lovely ripe, honeyed nose with age, almost Germanic,

with rich, floral, raisiny ripeness. Crisp, steely acidity on the palate, very long, powerful, with very pure varietal flavour, and tremendous length. Very concentrated wine, which needs at least 5-6 years and has the potential for almost unlimited ageing.
See also Vendange Tardive

MARC KREYDENWEISS, Andlau
Propriétaire viticulteur
Andlau Riesling (1983/84/85/86) ①

The basic generic Riesling from this property, which includes wine from the young vines on Kastelberg. Very delicate, herbaceous, sappy young wine, floral, appley when young, with firm fruit, and very clean, racy acidity to balance. Very grassy, herbal fruit, which evolves well, and needs at least 3-5 years ageing. Delicate, highly-strung style. Good value.

Grand Cru Wiebelsberg
(1969/79/81/82/83/84/85/86) ② / ③ ★★

Soft, gentle, floral style, lightweight, very elegant, with herbal, spicy aromas. Never heavy or aggressive, with smoky, spicy ripe fruit flavours, which require several years' ageing. Keep at least 3-5 years, and will evolve over many more years. Picked late in 1985 and 1986, with a more peachy, floral, honeyed fruit. Capable of very long ageing. Very clean.
Grand Cru Kastelberg (1969/71/82-87) ③ ★★★
Very steely, gunflint style, dry, austere, requiring several years

before it even starts to show its potential. Very minerally, flinty, dry wine with great breeding, and a clean, lemony, almost aggressive acidity when young, when it is very closed. Needs keeping at least 6-10 years even in lesser vintages, whilst the top vintages require 15 years or more. Capable of almost limitless ageing.

See also Vendange Tardive

KUENTZ-BAS, Husseren-les-Châteaux
Négociant
Cuvée Tradition (1986) ☒

Attractive, light, floral nose. Clean, fresh riesling fruit on palate, with quite marked acidity, and good length of young, mineral, riesling fruit. Clean, well-made. A wine for medium term keeping. 4-6+ years.

GÉRARD LANDMANN, Nothalten
Propriétaire viticulteur
Grand Cru Muenchberg (1986) ☒

Very attractive, floral riesling nose, lightweight, minerally but a little marred by sulphur on nose and palate. Quite lean, lightweight, dry, with good acidity to balance. Attractive, a little short. Keep 4-5 years from vintage.

LANDMANN OSTHOLT, Soultzmatt
Propriétaire viticulteur
Generic (1983) ☒

Rather sour, sulphury fruit, with a hint of soft, mature, oily Riesling. Very disappointing. Not recommended.

JÉROME LORENTZ, Bergheim
Négociant
Cuvée des Templiers (1985) ☒

Light, fresh, floral riesling nose and palate, good varietal flavour, lightweight, pleasant. A little short, but quite attractive.

PHILIPPE LORENTZ, Traenheim
Propriétaire viticulteur
Grand Cru Altenberg de Bergbieten (1985) ☒ ★

Pronounced aromatic, floral nose. Very clean, fresh, lightweight riesling fruit, pure flavour, well-balanced, with elegant, light, spicy flavour. Medium term keeping. 4-8+ years.

JEAN LUC MADER, Hunawihr
Propriétaire viticulteur
Grand Cru Rosacker (1985/86) ②

Quite appley nose in its youth, fresh, sappy, floral. Very fresh, light, minerally fruit on the palate, lightweight, very fresh, with medium length of flavour and good varietal flavour. Clean, fresh, dry, for medium term keeping. 4-6+ years.

FRÉDÉRIC MALLO, Hunawihr
Propriétaire viticulteur
Generic (1985/86) ① / ②

Clean, soft, gentle, herbaceous style, slightly off-dry, with medium length of fruit. Good varietal flavours, lightweight style.

Grand Cru Rosacker (1983/84/85/86) ② / ③ ★

Very steely, minerally, herbal fruit, which develops a lovely, honeyed, petrol character with age. Flinty, smoky, ripe fruit, with good balancing acidity. Not unapproachable when young, but develops well, and should be kept at least 5-7 years, with good potential for further ageing. Lovely, spicy, cinnamon richness in good vintages.

See also Vendange Tardive

HUBERT METZ, Blienschwiller
Propriétaire viticulteur
Generic (1986) ②

Young, fresh, sappy, confectionery nose. Fresh, clean, youthful,

floral, appley fruit on the palate, lightweight, a little short, but very clean. Delicate style of wine for medium term keeping. 3-6 years.

FRÉDÉRIC MOCHEL, Traenheim
Propriétaire viticulteur
Grand Cru Altenberg de Bergbieten (1985) 2️⃣

Fresh, floral, appley nose and palate, but with a slight yeastiness on the finish, a little short. Gentle, light fruit, soft, delicate style. Disappointing finish.

Grand Cru Altenberg de Bergbieten, Cuvée Henrietta (1985) ② / ③ ★

The top cuvée. Sappy, floral, young nose and palate, with more positive weight of fruit, and a broader, more floral, spicy flavour. Good balancing acidity, with quite fat finish, and good length of very clean riesling flavour. Needs 4-6 years keeping.

JULES MULLER, Bergheim
Négociant
La Dame au Faucon (1986) ②

Quite developed nose, even when young. Fresh, youthful fruit on the palate, with quite positive acidity, and ripe, long flavour, which will develop well. Very clean, quite lean, dry, with good varietal character. Good ageing potential.

MURÉ, CLOS ST. LANDELIN, Rouffach
Négociant
Clos St. Landelin (1983/85) ②

Very dumb on nose and palate when young, needs 4-5 years to develop. Quite broad, honeyed, soft, spicy fruit on palate, a little clumsy, almondy. Medium length of flavour. Pleasant, but without concentration.

DOMAINE OSTERTAG, Epfig
Propriétaire viticulteur
Vignoble d'Epfig (1985/86/87) ②

Clean, crisp, floral nose, with lean, young, almost appley fruit when first bottled. Elegant, very clean, lightweight. Good varietal flavour. Keep 3-5+ years.

Heissenberg (1986/87) ② ★

From a warm, granite slope. 1986 was the first vintage from this vineyard. Softer, riper, more floral fruit, with hints of mango. Quite light structure, with good ripeness and quite rapid development. Very clean, well-made.

Fronholtz (1985/87) ② ★

Lemony, steely acidity, less 'charming' when young. Harder wine, lean, quite minerally, needing longer ageing. Fresh, quite austere character. Keep 5-7+ years. Good potential for long ageing.

Grand Cru Muenchberg (1983/84/85/87) ② / ③ ★★

Quite powerful steely structure, hard to taste when young, but developing lovely rich, slightly petrolly riesling fruit with age. Very lean, dry, with good weight of steely fruit, and quite hard acidity in its youth, which gives it great potential for ageing. Very clean, pure, well-made wine. Keep for at least 5-8+ years.

PFLUGER-HAEGEL, Dambach-la-Ville
Propriétaire viticulteur
1986 ☐1 / ☐2

Spicy, slightly almondy, vanilla nose, attractive, but not varietal. Soft, mild, gentle fruit on the palate, with a hint of baked almonds. A little short, soft and lacking intensity. Pleasant, but not very varietal.

PREISS HENNY, Mittelwihr
Négociant
Cuvée Marcel Preiss (1981) ☐3

Light, honeyed, oily riesling nose and palate, spicy fruit, soft, with good varietal character, and medium length. Slightly cardboardy finish, but otherwise pleasant, attractive.

PREISS ZIMMER, Riquewihr
Négociant
Generic (1986) ☐1

Light, aromatic nose. Soft, lightweight fruit on the palate, a little short, anonymous, but pleasant. Quite good varietal flavour, but lacks weight.

Année Exceptionelle (1983) ☐2 ★

Soft, honeyed nose, marred by slight sulphur. Good varietal

character on palate, with a little residual sugar, and a slight,
sweet, raisiny finish. Good length of flavour, slight spritz, nicely
developed, soft, ripe Riesling. A little broad, soft, but attractive.

JULIEN RIEFFEL, Mittelbergheim
Propriétaire viticulteur
Brandluft (1986)   ① / ②
Undeveloped nose, with clean, light, sappy, herbal fruit on the
palate. Elegant, well-balanced, quite sappy, but a little short.
Pleasant, well-made.
Brandluft Réserve (1986)   ②
Fatter, richer style of fruit than the above, with good balancing
acidity, and a longer finish. Medium weight, fresh, clean,
well-made. For medium term keeping. 4-6+ years.
Zotzenberg (1986)   ① / ② ★
More pronounced nose, with drier, leaner crisper fruit on the
palate. Lightweight, with a slight spritz. Fresh, herbal, almost
grassy. Very clean. For medium term keeping. 4-6 years.
See also Vendange Tardive

ROLLY GASSMANN, Rorschwihr
Propriétaire viticulteur
Réserve Millésime (1983/84)   ② ★/★★
Attractive light, lean fruit, very clean, and with a rich, oily

VIN D'ALSACE

Rolly Gassmann

Riesling

APPELLATION ALSACE CONTROLEE

PRODUCE OF FRANCE   Mis en bouteille à la propriété   70 cl

ROLLY GASSMANN PROPRIÉTAIRES-VITICULTEURS
RORSCHWIHR (HAUT-RHIN) FRANCE

pungency in 1983. The '84 had rather too much acidity for the fruit, but both vintages showed a purity of varietal character and a good length of flavour.

SOCIÉTÉ VINICOLE ST. ODILE, Obernai
Co-operative
Clos Sainte Odile (1985) ②

Quite evolved oily riesling nose. Rather sour, cardboardy fruit on the palate, with some varietal flavour, but rather soapy, unpleasant. Not recommended.

DOMAINE MARTIN SCHAETZEL, Ammerschwihr
Propriétaire viticulteur
Cuvée Réserve (1985) ②

Slightly cheesy nose and palate, almondy, artificial, with little riesling character. Maybe an unfortunate bottle, but not very pleasant.

CHARLES SCHLERET, Turckheim
Propriétaire viticulteur
Cuvée Réserve (1984) ②

Honeyed nose of the '84 vintage. Clean, light, fresh, riesling fruit on the palate, delicate, herbal, very clean. Medium length. Well-made wine, elegant. Medium term keeping. 4-6 years.

DOMAINES SCHLUMBERGER, Guebwiller
Propriétaire viticulteur
Princes Abbés (1986) ②

Generally made from the young Grand Cru vines, less than 10 years old. Light, soft, broad, perfumed fruit, with crisp, slightly citric finish. Fresh, floral, with nice balance, quite lightweight. Medium term keeping. 3-5 years.

Grand Cru Saering (1983/85) ② ★

Soft style, dry but quite broad, full-bodied, with ripe, grapey, riesling character, and floral, warm, gentle fruit. Quite earthy, sometimes heavy. Keep 4-7 years from vintage, potential for longer ageing.

Grand Cru Kitterlé (1981/83/84/85) ③ ★/★★

Develops a lovely peachy, petrolly, aromatic nose with age. Quite slaty, oily, with rich, broad, earthy, powerful fruit. Rather dumb when young, needing at least 5 years, and capable of ageing much longer. Good balancing acidity, giving pronounced petrolly gunflint character with age.

ROLAND SCHMITT, Bergbieten
Propriétaire viticulteur
Grand Cru Altenberg de Bergbieten (1985/86) ☐2 ★★
Very minerally, floral nose, fresh, youthful. Lean, dry, minerally fruit on the palate, with good balancing acidity, and nice steely, firm structure. Herbal delicacy, with ripe fruit, firm, well structured. Medium to long term keeping. 5-8+ years.

RENÉ SCHMIDT, Riquewihr
Négociant
Grand Cru Schoenenberg, Cuvée Particulière (1985)
Initially attractive, light, petrolly riesling nose, but marred by
sulphur. Rather dull, disappointing fruit on the palate, flat, a
little sulphury, without much length or character. Not
recommended.

ALBERT SCHOECH, Ammerschwihr
Propriétaire viticulteur
Generic (1985)   ☑
Soft, ripe, petrolly riesling nose and palate, quite rich, ripe, with
solid fruit and good balancing acidity, spicy, gently rounded,
with quite good length. A little marred by sulphur on nose and
palate.

MAURICE SCHOECH, Ammerschwihr
Propriétaire viticulteur
Generic (1985)   ☱ / ☑
Clean, light, quite spicy fruit, dry, but quite soft, with light
balancing acidity. Good length of well-balanced flavour, for
medium term keeping. 4-7 years.
Kaefferkopf (1986)   ☑ ★
Light, floral, appley nose and palate, with clean, lively, fresh
young fruit, and a hint of residual sugar. Medium length of
flavour, fresh, lean, quite herbaceous. Medium term keeping.
3-6 years.

SCHROEDEL SARL (same firm as VEUVE JOSEPH PFISTER and J. B. ADAM), Sigolsheim
Négociant
Florimont (1986)   ☱ / ☑
Very floral, spicy, elderflower nose, fragrant, fresh. Clean, crisp,
lightweight fruit on the palate, attractive, fresh, well-balanced.
For drinking quite young. 3-6 years.
Réserve (1985)   ☱
Softer, rounder, more earthy style, with less pronounced nose.
Gentle, fatter, broader, with a rather short finish. Pleasant,
unexciting.

PAUL SCHWACH, Ribeauvillé
Propriétaire viticulteur
Generic (1985)   ☱
Quite high acidity on the palate overpowers the light fruit.

Rather artificial, not very interesting. Lacks varietal character.
Not recommended.

SICK-DREYER, Ammerschwihr
Propriétaire viticulteur
Kaefferkopf (1984/85) ② ★

Light, spicy, floral, quite broad style, with floral minerally fruit,
developing a hint of petrol after 3-4 years. Medium weight, quite
soft style, for medium term keeping. 4-7 years.

VIN D'ALSACE
APPELLATION ALSACE CONTRÔLEE
RIESLING

Kaefferkopf

750ml *Sick Dreyer* ®

Mis en bouteille par
R.SICK·P.DREYER·PROP.VITICULTEURS·AMMERSCHWIHR (Ht RHIN)
PRODUIT DE FRANCE – PRODUCE OF FRANCE

CAVE CO-OPÉRATIVE DE SIGOLSHEIM, Sigolsheim
Co-operative
Kaefferkopf (1985) ②

Light, clean fruit on the palate, well-balanced, rather solid, flat,
and a little lacking in charm. Slightly cardboardy finish. Quite
good varietal character, correct, but unexciting.

JEAN SIPP, Ribeauvillé
Propriétaire viticulteur
Generic (1984) ①

The generic wine is made in lesser vintages. Pleasant, light,
minerally fruit, fresh, sappy, clean, a little short.

Réserve (1985) ☐2

Fresh, clean, young, sappy fruit, fragrant, medium weight, quite soft, easy drinking, without great length. Medium term keeping. 4-6 years.

Grand Cru Kirchberg de Ribeauvillé (1985/83/86) ☐2 / ☐3 ★

Ripe, powerful, floral fruit, which develops petrolly aromas after 5 years, with clean, positive fruit on the palate, ripe, full flavoured, with good varietal character, balancing acidity and a hint of residual richness. Medium to long term keeping. 5-8+ years.

LOUIS SIPP, Ribeauvillé
Négociant
Grand Cru Kirchberg de Ribeauvillé (1983) ☐2

Quite oily, developed riesling nose. Ripe, broad riesling fruit on the palate, a little heavy, dull. Good weight of flavour, with some balancing acidity, but a little lifeless, with a slightly dull finish. Disappointing for the vintage.

PIERRE SPARR & SES FILS, Sigolsheim
Négociant
Altenbourg Cuvée Centenaire (1981) ☐3

Mature, soft, buttery riesling nose and palate, raisiny, positive, quite soft and rich. Quite sweet finish. Gentle riesling fruit, quite soft, mature, drinking very well now. Attractive, at its peak.

Grand Cru Schlossberg (1985) ☐3

Fresh, floral nose. Dry, minerally, lean style, young crisp and

fresh, with medium weight of fruit, and good balancing acidity. A little residual sugar. A little lacking the concentration of a Grand Cru. Medium term ageing. 4-7+ years.

CAVES PH. J. SPENER, Ribeauvillé

Co-operative

Generic (1985/86) ☐

Light, soft fruit, rather bland, with a little varietal character, but rather lightweight, anonymous and a little flat, sulphury, dull. Acceptable but uninspiring.

JEAN-BAPTISTE THOMANN & FILS, Ammerschwihr
Propriétaire viticulteur
Generic (1984/85)   ☑

> Very clean, attractive well-made light, herbal wine, lightweight,
> but very correct, well-balanced, with good varietal character.
> For drinking young. 3-6 years.

Cuvée Jean-Baptiste (1985/86)   ☑

> Made in good vintages only. Crisp, light fruit, lightweight, fresh,
> with good riesling character, but a rather short finish. Floral,
> sappy, very light. For medium term keeping. 4-6 years.

Kaefferkopf (1986)   ☑

> Young, herbal, grassy, hessian nose. Youthful, appley riesling
> fruit, lightweight, with a hint of residual sugar. Pleasant,
> medium length, for medium term keeping. 4-6 years.

F. E. TRIMBACH, Ribeauvillé
Négociant
Generic (1983/84/85)   ☑

> Youthful, delicate riesling fruit, dry, fresh, quite lightweight.
> Very clean fruit, with light acidity, and medium length. Nose
> develops within 2-3 years, palate 4-5 years. Medium term
> keeping. 4-6+ years.

Réserve (1983/5)   ☑ ★

> Made in good vintages only. More powerful, ripe fruit, which
> develops flinty, petrolly aromas with 4-6 years, capable of being
> kept much longer. Very clean, well-made. Recommended.

Cuvée Frédéric Emile (1982/83/85) ③ ★★

More backward style. Richer and more concentrated fruit,
honeyed, spicy, mellow, soft, generous. Still dry, but with a
smoky richness and ripeness, and firm balancing acidity.
Broader, richer structure, which ages very well, taking on an
oily, petrolly maturity. Made from their own vines, this is a very
reliable wine in all vintages, with medium to long term ageing
ability. 5-10+ years.

Clos Sainte Hune (1971/76/77/78/81/82) ④ / ⑤ ★★★

The flagship wine of Trimbach, produced in tiny quantities in
their vineyard in Hunawihr by the Grand Cru Rosacker. This
wine always takes a long time to mature, and is only released in
its sixth year, although it needs a good deal longer. Very
powerful, smoky, steely flavour, with almost citric acidity and a
lovely clean balance. Develops rich, petrolly, gunflint aromas
with age and is capable of very long ageing. Keep 8-20+ years.

CAVE VINICOLE DE TURCKHEIM, Turckheim

Co-operative

Cave Tradition (1986) ①

Light floral nose, gentle. Ripe, floral, spicy fruit on the palate,
not heavy, but with good length of ripe flavour. Fresh, youthful,
appley fruit, with clean balancing acidity, and medium length.
Good value. Medium term keeping. 3-6+ years.

La Decapole (1983) ②

Their better cuvée made in good vintages. Raisin-like ripe fruit of
the vintage, rich, almost peachy, gentle, ripe, tropical fruits. Less
varietal character, but very seductive, attractive, with gentle acidity
and good length of very soft, ripe fruit. Almost late-harvest style.

R. WACH & FILS, Andlau
Propriétaire viticulteur
Grand Cru Moenchberg (1983)

   Honeyed nose, not very varietal, a little cardboardy. Medium
   weight of fruit, soft, a little disappointing, although it develops
   quite well in the glass. Medium length of quite light, gentle fruit,
   for short to medium term keeping. 5-8 years.

MAISON WIEDERHIRN, Riquewihr
Propriétaire viticulteur
Coteau du Schoenenberg Réserve Personelle (1985)   ③

Oily, flinty riesling nose and palate, with good lemony, smoky acidity, and good weight of fruit. A little closed at present, but with good balance and length. Keep for 5-8 years.
See also Vendange Tardive

ALSACE WILLM, Barr
Négociant
Generic (1985)   [1]

Fresh, sappy, herbal riesling nose and palate, pleasant, lightweight, without strong character, but very pleasant. For drinking young and fresh. 3-5 years.

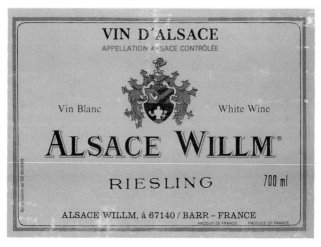

WOLFBERGER, Eguisheim
Co-operative
Cuvée St. Leon IX (1983)   [3]

The top Riesling cuvée. Attractive, petrolly riesling nose, but rather high, hard acidity on the palate, without the fruit to balance. Ripe, fat riesling fruit, rather dull, flat, and disappointing. Overpriced for the quality. Beautiful presentation, shame about the wine.

DOMAINE ZIND HUMBRECHT, Wintzenheim
Propriétaire viticulteur
Generic (1985/86/87)   [1] / [2]

Young, sappy riesling fruit, quite herbal, green fruits. Very fresh, clean, quite lightweight, with good varietal character. Made from the younger vines. Medium term ageing. Keep 4-6 years.

Herrenweg (1971/85/86/87)   [3] ★★

Very floral, perfumed, aromatic wine, which comes round relatively early. Good positive weight of fruit, powerful, lean, elegant, with more grape character than soil character. Minerally, powerful, clean riesling fruit, which develops well after 4-5 years, although can last far beyond that as witnessed by a brilliant 1971 tasted recently, which had rich, buttery fruit and a superb length of intense gunflint, petrolly riesling flavour. Superb quality wines, well worth the price.

Clos Hauserer (1985/86/87)   [2] / [3] ★

The heavy clay soil of this vineyard gives wines that take a long time to mature and are often ungenerous when young. The 1983 now has a lovely smoky, powerful, pungent nose, with rich, flinty fruit on the palate. This vineyard never gives heavy wines, but they are always very powerful, taking on a petrolly aroma with age. Long term keeping. 6-10+ years.

Grand Cru Rangen (1983/85/86/87) ③ ★★

Broad, earthy, aromatic wines, with a pronounced *goût de terroir*, the result of the volcanic soil. Very powerful, minerally rich wines, full flavoured, with a fatter, broader style. Strongly individual wines. Long term ageing. Keep 6-10+ years.

Grand Cru Brand (1983/84/85/86/87) ③ ★★/★★★

Minerally, elegant, steely wine, less broad in style, leaner, a little lighter, with floral, grapey riesling character. Develops quite petrolly aromas with age. Very good concentration of flavours, very elegant and restrained. It is hard to choose a winner out of M. Humbrecht's three Grand Cru sites, but this would be my choice.

Grand Cru Hengst (1983/85/86/87) ③ ★

Fuller-bodied, more powerful wine, richer, more muscular, with rich, powerful ripe fruit flavours, almost smoky, spicy, fat, but always with good balancing acidity. Medium to long term keeping. 5-10+ years.

See also Vendange Tardive

RIESLING VENDANGE TARDIVE

JEAN BAPTISTE ADAM, Ammerschwihr
Négociant
Kaefferkopf, Cuvée Jean Baptiste (1983) ③

Attractive, oily riesling nose. Rich, concentrated fruit, powerful, dry, steely, with excellent balance. Very closed, needs long keeping. Good value for Vendange Tardive. Very good ageing potential. Keep 12-20+ years.

DOMAINE LUCIEN ALBRECHT, Orschwihr
Propriétaire viticulteur
Grand Cru Pfingstberg Vendange Tardive (1985/83) ④ ★★
Distinctive, elegant, flinty, minerally nose, just starting to develop. Very clean, minerally steely fruit, firm, dry, powerful, with very good balancing acidity and tremendous power. Excellent potential. Needs very long ageing. Keep at least 10-20+ years.

DOMAINE MARCEL DEISS (Jean Michel Deiss), Bergheim
Propriétaire viticulteur
Vendange Tardive Bergheim Burg (1983) ④

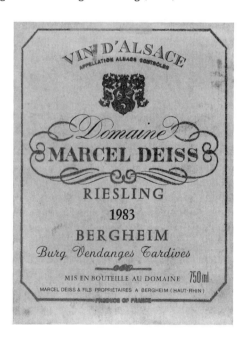

Quite developed, buttery riesling nose, oily, fat, rich. Quite high acidity on palate, with rich fruit and soft, buttery ripeness. Attractive, rich balance of flavour, still quite undeveloped. Less powerful than many, but with nice balance. Keep 8-12+ years.

DOPFF AU MOULIN, Riquewihr
Négociant
Grand Cru Schoenenburg Vendange Tardive
(1983/81) ③ / ④ ★

Develops quite fast. The 1981 has a rich, developed, evolved riesling nose and palate, oily, quite fat, slightly flinty, with rich floral fruit, quite soft and ripe, at its best now. The 1983 still has plenty of life and will last comfortably until the year 2000. Very clean, ripe fruit, not heavy, but with good structure, and medium weight. Just starting to drink well now.

DOPFF & IRION, Riquewihr
Négociant
Vendanges Tardives (1982) ④ ★

Lively, developed, peachy, oily riesling nose. Very slaty, flinty, minerally Riesling on the palate, with lovely soft balancing acidity. Dry, honeyed, well-balanced, still quite rich, but drinking very well now. Very well-made.

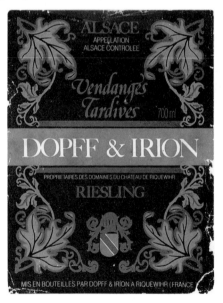

FALLER, DOMAINE WEINBACH, Kayserberg
Propriétaire viticulteur
Vendanges Tardives (1983) ⑤ ★★

From a patch of vines at the bottom of the Schlossberg vineyard. Quite pale colour. Lovely smoky, flinty, riesling nose, rich, concentrated, ripe riesling fruit, with good balancing acidity and a little residual sugar. Quite broad, floral fruit, with hints of oily botrytis. Very clean, concentrated, with long firm finish. Long ageing potential. Keep at least 10 years.

HUGEL & FILS, Riquewihr
Négociant
Vendange Tardive, Sélection Personelle Jean Hugel (1981/83/85) ④ / ⑤

Often dumb when young, this wine develops rich, fat, broad, floral, smoky, oily fruit. Dry, but with great power and richness of flavour. Keep 6-10+ years, with potential for very long ageing. 1976 tasted recently was still fresh, clean and just commencing its development.

ANDRÉ KIENTZLER, Ribeauvillé
Propriétaire viticulteur
Grand Cru Geisberg Vendange Tardive (1983) ④ ★★

Quite herbal, spicy, floral nose, still undeveloped. Ripe, rich fatness of the vintage, with spicy, almost smoky, grassy flavours. Still closed, undeveloped, with lovely long, clean fruit. Quite rich, muscular style. Needs long ageing. Keep 10-15+ years. Also made in 1985.

'Vin de Glace' Osterberg (1986) ⑤ ★★

Full straw colour. Intense, honeyed, rich, concentrated riesling fruit, rich, raisiny, with good balancing acidity. Very honeyed style, off-dry, with intense concentration of flavour. Will probably start to come round in the mid-1990s.

MARC KREYDENWEISS, Andlau
Propriétaire viticulteur
Grand Cru Kastelberg Vendange Tardive (1985)   ④ ★★★
Restrained floral, herbal, minerally nose. Very long, steely fruit on the palate, still very closed, with powerful, flinty, smoky fruit and long, intensely ripe fruit. Very intense varietal character, ripe, with a touch of honey. A wine for very long keeping. Keep at least 10-15 years, with the potential for unlimited ageing.

FRÉDÉRIC MALLO, Hunawihr
Propriétaire viticulteur
Grand Cru Rosacker Vendange Tardive (1985)   ③ / ④ ★
Rich honey and confectionery nose. Good length of ripe, soft, almost raisiny/honeyed fruit, with lovely acid balance. Good length of flavour, more forward than many, but will still improve with further ageing. Keep 5-10 years, with potential for longer ageing.

JULIEN RIEFFEL, Mittelbergheim
Propriétaire viticulteur
Vendange Tardive (1985)   ③ / ④ ★
Honeyed, ripe, grapey, raisiny nose, not very developed. Clean, rich, dry fruit on palate, with good balancing acidity. Clean, still

very closed, youthful, with secondary aromas just starting.
Lovely clean, ripe riesling flavour. Keep 6-10 years, with good
potential for longer ageing.

MAISON WIEDERHIRN, Riquewihr
Propriétaire viticulteur
Coteau de Schoenenberg Vendanges Tardives (1983)　⑤ ★
　Baked, raisiny nose, undeveloped at present. Ripe fruit on the
　palate, with good riesling flavour, and clean, steely, balancing
　acidity. Rather steely, powerful structure, still quite closed.
　Well-balanced, firm, dry, with rich riesling finish. Keep at least
　10 years, with excellent potential for longer ageing.

DOMAINE ZIND HUMBRECHT, Wintzenheim
Propriétaire viticulteur

Grand Cru Brand Vendange Tardive (1983)　⑤ ★★
　Quite developed nose, rich, perfumed, aromatic. Soft, ripe, firm
　fruit on the palate, powerful, dry, rich, oily complex petrol
　Riesling, with steely balancing acidity. Clean, firm, with very
　long finish. Just starting to evolve. Keep 10+ years, with
　potential for very long ageing.

GEWURZTRAMINER

Gewurztraminer is a particularly aromatic clone of the Traminer grape, originally from Tramin in the Italian Tyrol, which appears to have been introduced into Alsace via the Rheinpfalz. There are mentions of a particularly spicy grape, which would seem to have been the Gewurztraminer, in Alsace from the sixteenth century, and the Traminer is mentioned by the botanist Bock in the Kreuterbuch, published in 1551. The variety has been known under a number of names: Traminer Musqué, Gentil Rose Aromatique, and Edeltraube, the name 'Gewurz' traminer, meaning literally spicy Traminer, first appearing in 1870. Earlier this century, many growers presented both a Traminer and a Gewurztraminer, the latter being the more heavily spicy of the two. It is said to have developed as a clonal selection, possibly as a result of Chrétien Oberlin's work on this subject in Colmar. Since January 1973 the name Traminer has been discontinued, except in a very small area of Alsace, which still produces wine from the Traminer, or Savagnin Rose, around the town of Heiligenstein, under the name of Klevener de Heiligenstein (p. 110–11).

Gewurztraminer is a moderate grower, requiring a long growing season, without which it can produce grapes that are too low in acidity and therefore lack balance. Budbreak is early and spring frosts can greatly reduce crops in some years. Ripening is mid-season and grapes left on the vines late into the autumn can easily ripen to Vendange Tardive or Sélection de Grains Nobles in good vintages.

Around 2,485 hectares of Gewurztraminer are planted, representing an average of 15 per cent to 20 per cent of the wine produced in Alsace. The crop size varies considerably with vintage variations and, on average, Gewurztraminer gives the lowest yield of all the varieties grown in Alsace. The larger proportion of Gewurztraminer is grown in the Haut Rhin. It is not too fussy about soil or aspect, but is highly susceptible to grey rot.

Gewurztraminer is the most easily recognised of the Alsace varieties: it has a soft, warm, aromatic bouquet and flavour, reminiscent often of rosewater and turkish delight, sometimes with a touch of lychees. It is seldom high in acidity and is usually quite high in alcohol. It is often vinified with just a touch of residual sugar. It can occasionally be overpoweringly, almost cloyingly, over-perfumed and a good Gewurztraminer should have spicy fruit as well as perfume. In hot vintages, such as 1976 and 1983, Gewurztraminer can be too heavy for its own good, lacking the acidity to balance, therefore producing wines which age rapidly. In colder vintages, such as 1984, the problem can be lack of ripeness and the wines can lack the essential 'fatness' that is an integral part of the Gewurztraminer wine. Vintages such as 1985 are the ideal, providing the balance between fruit and acidity, and producing some very long-lived wines. But in all cases, the choice of producer is as important as the choice of vintage, as a good producer will be competent to get the best out of his grapes in any given vintage.

Gewurztraminers range from the light and elegant wines, discreetly spicy, which can be served as aperitifs, or with fish or chicken, to richer, more powerful wines that could partner cheeses (especially Munster, the local speciality). The heavier wines are excellent with foie gras, lobster or smoked salmon, whilst the Alsaciens would serve these wines with the dessert. A plain fruit flan matches the richer-flavoured Gewurztraminers, but do not forget that most Vendange Tardive wines are medium to dry and are not ideal with strongly flavoured puddings or gâteaux. That would be a waste of both wine and food.

Vendange Tardive Gewurztraminers vary tremendously in style. The appellation lays down the minimum sugar level at harvest (243 grams per litre), but it does not lay down the law in the matter of residual sugar after fermentation. It is up to the individual producer to decide whether to ferment the wine to dryness, with an alcohol level of over 14°, or to stop the fermentation at around 12°, leaving a wine with residual sweetness. Unfortunately there is no indication on the label of which is the case.

In good vintages, Sélection de Grains Nobles is produced from Gewurztraminer grapes. This will be medium sweet to very sweet. The effect of the botrytis is often to minimise the varietal character of the grape, but Gewurztraminer usually retains a ripe grapefruit/lychee flavour. These wines often need keeping for 10 or even for 20 years.

As a general rule, basic inexpensive Gewurztraminers should be at their best between one to four years from the vintage; special selections, *réserve* cuvées, and single vineyard and Grand Cru wines between three to ten years, Vendange Tardive wines between five to 15 years, and Sélection de Grains Nobles between five and 20 years.

The skins and pips left over after pressing are used to produce one of Alsace's most famous Eaux-de-Vie: Marc de Gewurztraminer, which has its own Appellation Contrôlée and which retains the aromatic flavour of the grapes.

GEWURZTRAMINER

JEAN-BAPTISTE ADAM, Ammerschwihr
Négociant
Generic (1985) ☐2

Soft, floral, spicy, rosewater fruit, gentle, quite lightweight, floral but not earthy. Light varietal character, soft, well-balanced.
3-5 years.
See also Vendange Tardive

GASTON BECK, Zellenberg
Négociant
Generic (1985) ☐2

Soft, spicy nose, light, spicy fruit on the palate, a little sweet.
Gentle, fat, rosewater fruit, medium length, with good varietal

character. Pleasant, lightweight wine for drinking young.
2-5 years.

PRODUIT — DE FRANCE

VIN D'ALSACE
Appellation Alsace Contrôlée

GEWURZTRAMINER
13 % Vol.   70 cl
Mis en bouteille par *Gaston BECK* 68340 Zellenberg (France)

J. BECKER (same firm as above), Zellenberg
Négociant
Generic (1985) ☐2
  Soft, spicy fruit, gentle, not very positive. A little flat,
  cardboardy, rather lacking in varietal character. Unexciting.

LÉON BEYER, Eguisheim
Négociant
Generic (1985/86) ☐1 / ☐2
  Very clean, gently spicy, elegant, firm, not heavy. Very good,
  positive, varietal character, starts to develop quite young.
  Medium length of flavour, soft, well-balanced.
Réserve (1983/85) ☐2 / ☐3
  More minerally, earthy, richer fruit. Fat, powerful, spicy,
  grapefruit flavours, with clean acidity to balance. Rounder,
  full-flavoured wine, with more weight and power. Develops quite
  young. Keep 4-6+ years.
Cuvée des Comtes d'Eguisheim
(1967/69/81/82/83/85) ☐3 ★★★
  The top cuvée of Gewurztraminer, with a more steely backbone,
  and broader, bigger structure. Marc Beyer refers to the vineyard
  which produces this wine as the 'Côte de Nuits' of Alsace,
  producing wines which take a long time to develop. Before 1964
  this cuvée was sold as Cuvée St. Leon. Develops ripe, buttery,

oily richness, with complex grapefruit flavour. Needs at least
5 years, and can continue to develop for many more years.
See also Vendange Tardive

EMILE BOECKEL, Mittelbergheim
Négociant
Generic (1985) ☐2

Very ripe nose, overripe mangos, guavas. Rather overblown

fruit, a little flat, heavy, with less varietal character. A little clumsy, dull.

Réserve (1985) ☐2

Rosewater, soft pineapple nose. Soft, spicy ripe fruit on the palate, pineappley, with some residual sugar. Medium weight, quite elegant, rather soft, ripe, gentle fruit, with good varietal character. For drinking young. 3-5 years.

Zotzenberg (1985) ☐2 ★

Rosewater, spicy nose, floral. Cleaner, lighter fruit on the palate, gently spicy, but more elegant, floral, less earthy. Good length of lightweight, floral, lychee fruit, for drinking young. 3-6 years.

BOTT FRÈRES, Ribeauvillé

Propriétaire viticulteur

Réserve Exceptionelle (1981/85) ☐3

Soft, warm, rosewater, spicy nose and palate, bitter grapefruit, gentle, round, with a hint of residual sweetness. Gentle, floral, quite lightweight. Soft, gentle fruit. For drinking young. 3-6 years.

Réserve Personelle (1983/85) ☐3 ★

Their top selection. Quite rich, spicy fruit, buttery, rich, with a ripe, raisiny, late harvest ripeness to the 1983. A little residual sugar, with rich, earthy, fat, broad, spicy fruit. Not heavy, but with good weight and length. For medium term keeping. 5-7+ years.

See also Vendange Tardive

ALBERT BOXLER, Niedermorschwihr
Propriétaire viticulteur
Grand Cru Brand (1985)   ② / ③ ★
> Light, spicy, floral, 'turkish delight' nose. Gentle, light fruit on
> the palate, elegant, floral, lightweight, with clean varietal
> flavour. Attractive well-balanced wine, with medium term
> keeping ability. 5-8 years.

See also Vendange Tardive

F. BRUCKER (formerly A. Gaschy), Wettolsheim
Négociant
'Floral', Tête de Cuvée (1985)   ②
> Quite broad, heavy, fat, earthy, spicy fruit on nose and palate.
> More powerful, heavy structure, full-blown. Rich earthy fruit,
> not strongly varietal. Medium length of flavour. Medium term
> keeping. 5-7 years.

CAMILLE BUCHER & FILS, Hunawihr
Propriétaire viticulteur
Generic (1986)   ②
> Attractive, light, floral, spicy nose and palate, quite
> full-flavoured, rich, but dry, with good length of varietal flavour
> and slight earthiness. A little lean and ungenerous, but very
> pleasant, well-made wine. Medium term keeping. 4-6 years.

JOSEPH CATTIN, Voegtlinshoffen
Propriétaire viticulteur
Grand Cru Hatschbourg (1985)   ② / ③ ★
   Rich, fat, broad, spicy, rosewater spice. Earthy, fat, full blown.
   Ripe, very forward, attractive style, for medium term ageing.
   Fat, full-flavoured and satisfying.
See also Vendange Tardive

THÉO CATTIN ET FILS, Voegtlinshoffen
Négociant
Bollenberg (1986)   ② ★

Light, undeveloped, spicy nose. Leaner, more floral, spicy fruit, lychees, smoky, spicy, medium weight of attractive elegant fruit. Good varietal character. Well-made. Medium term keeping ability. 4-8 years.
See also Vendange Tardive

DOMAINE MARCEL DEISS (Jean Michel Deiss), Bergheim
Propriétaire viticulteur
Mittelwihr (1986)   ②
Soft, rich, honeyed, spicy nose. Not a lot of body, pleasant, with a hint of residual sugar. Easy drinking, light, floral, fresh, with gentle, floral spice. For drinking young. 3-6 years.
Bergheim (1986)   ② ★
Broader, spicy fruit on nose and palate, very perfumed, cachous, rosewater, not heavy, but more powerfully structured. Good length of rich, spicy fruit, good varietal character.
Well-balanced, more interesting wine. For medium term keeping. 5-8+ years.

St. Hippolyte (1986)   ②
Soft, gentle, spicy nose, with broad, soft, earthy fruit, smoky, tobacco, broad, floral fruit, and slight sweetness on the finish.

Earthy richness, good varietal character. Medium term keeping.
4-6 years.

JEAN PIERRE DIRLER Bergholtz
Propriétaire viticulteur
Grand Cru Spiegel (1985)   ☑ ★
Youthful, floral, spicy nose. Gentle, quite soft, restrained fruit on
the palate, with good varietal character, but not too heavy.
Restrained, well balanced style, very floral and gentle. For
medium term keeping. 4-7 years.

DOPFF & IRION, Riquewihr
Négociant
Les Sorcières (1985)   ☑ ★
Light, spicy, rosewater nose, very aromatic. Aromatic, spicy fruit
on the palate, quite firm, with good weight of flavour and good
varietal character. A nice balance of rosewater, floral fruit and
ripe, grapey fatness. Medium term keeping. 4-8 years.

DOMAINE EHRHART, Ammerschwihr
Négociant
Domaine Ehrhart (1985)   ★
Positive, rich, grapefruit, lychee nose. Floral, full-flavoured, soft,
attractive, spicy fruit on the palate, lively, well balanced, with
good follow-through. A little residual sugar. Good classic varietal

flavour, good length of fruit. Elegant, well balanced. Medium term keeping. 3-5 years.

FÉLIX EPPELÉ, Ammerschwihr
Propriétaire viticulteur
Kaefferkopf (1985)   ☐1 / ☐2

Nose and palate of oxidised apples, with no varietal character. Probably gone through malolactic, but lacks recognisable varietal characteristics. Not recommended.

FALLER, DOMAINE WEINBACH, Kayserberg
Propriétaire viticulteur
Cuvée Laurence (1986)   ☐4 ★

Lovely full-blown varietal nose, hints of lychees, tobacco, rosewater. Rich, quite lean fruit on palate, rosewater, ripe, discreetly spicy fruit, with good length and balance. Very classic, well made wine, attractive young, but capable of ageing. 3-8 years.
See also Vendange Tardive

LOUIS FREYBURGER ET FILS, Bergheim
Propriétaire viticulteur
Grand Cru Altenberg de Bergheim (1983)   ☐2 ★

Light, delicate, floral nose, roses, wallflowers. Rich, warm, spicy fruit on the palate, medium weight, well-balanced, floral rather than spicy. Good ageing potential. 5-10 years.

LUCIEN FREYERMUTH, Dambach-la-Ville
Négociant
Generic (1985/86)   ① / ②

Quite fat, honeyed, raisiny, rich, spicy fruit, rather fat, honeyed, full blown in style, a little perfumed. A little lacking in body, but pleasant lightweight style, more perfume than spicy. For drinking young. 3-5 years.

VICTOR GAERTNER, Ammerschwihr
Propriétaire viticulteur
Kaefferkopf (1986)   ① / ②

Quite heavy, full-blown spicy earthy fruit, with minerally soil character. More solid, heavy, with less charm. For lovers of rich spicy Gewurztraminer. Medium keeping ability. 4-8 years.

JÉROME GESCHICKT, Ammerschwihr
Propriétaire viticulteur
Kaefferkopf (1985/86)   ② / ③ ★

Light, minerally, floral nose, with drier, more serious, earthy, mineral fruit on the palate. Quite broad, smoky, spicy fruit. Medium term keeping. 5-8 years.
See also Vendange Tardive

PAUL GINGLINGER, Eguisheim
Propriétaire viticulteur
Grand Cru Eichberg (1983/85) ② ★

Soft, rich, gently spicy fruit, with a broad, oily fatness and very good length of flavour. Elegant, not too heavy, with quite powerful, well-structured fruit, capable of medium to long term ageing. 5-8+ years.

LOUIS GISSELBRECHT, Dambach-la-Ville
Négociant
Generic (1985) ②

Quite rich, sweet, raisiny, spicy fruit on the palate, solid, quite soft, with little acidity. Quite full-flavoured, with good varietal character, but maybe a little too solid. Medium term keeping. 3-6 years.

WILLY GISSELBRECHT, Dambach-la-Ville
Négociant
Réserve Spéciale (1986) ① ★

Light, floral, almost sweet, spicy nose, cinnamon. Quite positive, rich, dry, spicy fruit on the palate, earthy, full flavoured, but very clean and not overwhelming. Well-balanced, with good varietal character. Medium term keeping. 3-6 years.

Médaille d'Or (1985/86) ② ★

Soft, gentle, ripe fruit, with a hint of residual sugar. Easier drinking style, grapey, fresh, turkish delight/rosewater. Good weight, with balancing acidity. Medium term keeping. 4-8 years.
See also Vendange Tardive

ANDRÉ & REMY GRESSER, Andlau
Propriétaire viticulteur
Andlau (1985) ☐2

Soft, sweet, coconut nose. Ripe, sweet, spicy fruit on the palate, more varietal on palate than on the nose. A little residual sugar. The sweetness rather overpowers the weight of fruit, but a very attractive elegant wine in the sweeter style.

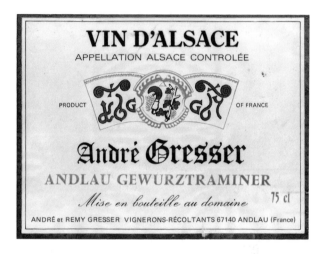

JEAN HEYWANG, Heiligenstein
Propriétaire viticulteur
Affenberg (1986) ☐2 ★

Soft, spicy, ripe, smoky fruit, gentle, dry, elegant, very clean. Well-balanced lean wine, with elegant well-balanced fruit and good varietal character. Medium term keeping. 3-6 years.

Grand Cru Kirchberg de Barr (1983/82/85) ☐2 ★

Very elegant, soft, spicy fruit, floral, minerally, with firm backbone and good length of flavour. Ripe, peachy, apricot fruit, not overwhelmingly spicy and quite slow to evolve. 1979 tasted recently had a lovely nutty evolved flavour, with no signs of age. Medium to long term keeping. 5-10+ years.

BARON DE HOEN, Beblenheim
Co-operative
Cuvée Particulière (1985) ☐2

Sweetish, spicy nose. Gentle, warm fruit on the palate, tinned grapefruit, some earthiness, with a little residual sugar. Pleasant, without any great concentration. Easy drinking. For drinking young. 3-5 years.

Grand Cru Sonnenglanz (1983)   [2] ★

Soft, gently spicy nose and palate, aromatic, cinnamon, gentle, earthy spice, very clean, elegant, restrained. Good length of flavour, firmer, lighter, less earthy style. Medium term keeping. 5-8 years.

HUGEL & FILS, Riquewihr
Négociant
Generic (1983/85/86) ☐2
Solid, broad, flowery wine, earthy, quite floral, with good weight of flavour. Gentle, quite broad, with medium length, for quite early drinking. Keep 2-4 years.
Cuvée Tradition (1985) ☐2 / ☐3
A little more depth of flavour, smoky, ripe fruit, broad, earthy, quite heavy voluptuous style. For lovers of big Gewurztraminers. Good length of flavour, for quite young drinking. 2-6 years.
Réserve Personelle (1983/85) ☐3 ★
Very muscular, solid style, with fat, ripe grapefruit aromas when young. Richer, more powerful fruit, longer flavour, and bigger structure, without being over-heavy. Quite closed when young, needs 5 years, and will continue to improve up to 10 years or more.

See also Vendange Tardive

JOSMEYER, Wintzenheim
Négociant

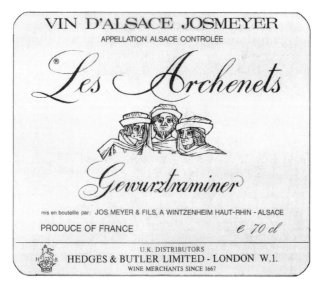

Les Archenets (1983/79) ☐2 ★
Big, powerful, earthy wine, dry but very full-flavoured, rich, with ripe grapefruit and lychees. Full-blown, rich, grapey style, for lovers of big Gewurztraminers. Very good length of flavour. Medium term keeping. 5-7 years.

ANDRÉ KIENTZLER, Ribeauvillé
Propriétaire viticulteur
Generic (1986) ☒ ★★
> Soft, rich, spicy, tobacco, rosewater nose and palate. Rich fruit, elegant, with very long flavour, quite minerally, restrained. A wine that needs ageing. Keep 5-7+ years.

See also Vendange Tardive

MARC KREYDENWEISS, Andlau
Propriétaire viticulteur
Kritt (1985/86/87) ☒ ★
> The Kritt vineyard is of glacial deposits and gives a lightweight, spicy, floral, rosewater wine, restrained, elegant, but never heavy. Quite lean, aromatic, grapey, for medium term keeping. Very well-balanced.

See also Vendange Tardive

KUENTZ BAS, Husseren-les-Châteaux
Négociant
Cuvée Tradition (1985) ☒
> Light, spicy, floral fruit, faded roses, slightly dull. Light varietal character, with some residual sugar. Medium length, pleasant, rather short.

See also Vendange Tardive

JÉROME LORENTZ, Bergheim
Négociant
Generic (1985) ☑
> Quite soft, fat, opulent spicy wine, grapey, with a little residual sweetness and a very floral perfumed fruit. Medium length, a little over-blown, lacking in concentration.

See also Vendange Tardive
Cuvée des Templiers (1985) ☑
> Gentle, rounded, spicy, rosewater fruit on the palate, clean, soft, with some residual sugar. Light varietal character, easy to drink, but a little dilute, sugar water, lacking body.

PHILIPPE LORENTZ, Bergbieten
Propriétaire viticulteur
Grand Cru Altenberg de Bergbieten (1985) ☑ / ☒
> Delicate, discreet, soft, rose nose. Clean, very lean, young, sappy, spicy fruit on the palate, lean, elegant, lightweight, with youthful astringency. Very clean varietal character, a wine for medium term keeping. 4-7 years.

FRÉDÉRIC MALLO, Hunawihr
Propriétaire viticulteur
Mandelberg (1986/85) ☑ ★
> A calcareous clay vineyard. Elegant, spicy nose, lightweight, with hints of herbs, parsley. Discreetly spicy on the palate, with a slight residual sugar, but with an impression of dryness,

firmness. Good length of elegant, balanced fruit, medium weight.
Medium term keeping. 5-8 years.

METZ FRÈRES, Ribeauvillé,
Négociant
Sélection Personelle (1985)   ① / ②
  Soft, warm, fruit nose and palate, gentle, quite pleasant, but
  lacking varietal character. Rather anonymous flavour, medium
  length. Not recommended.

HUBERT METZ, Blienschwiller
Propriétaire viticulteur
Winzenberg (1985/86)   ②
  Soft, sappy, rosewater fruit, grapefruity, gentle, with good initial
  flavour, but a little lacking in body. Pleasant, quite attractive,
  but a little short.

FRÉDÉRIC MOCHEL, Traenheim
Propriétaire viticulteur
Grand Cru Altenberg de Bergbieten (1985)   ②
  Light, floral, rose-petal nose. Aromatic, herbal, spicy, delicate
  style, lightweight, gently aromatic, leaner weight, quite forward.
  Well-made lighter style, for medium term keeping. 4-6 years.

JULES MULLER, Bergheim
Négociant
Generic (1986)   ②
  Light, aromatic, floral nose and palate, a little residual sugar,

light, fresh young fruit, with light balancing acidity. Medium length, soft, well-balanced, with good varietal character. For drinking young. 2-5 years.
See also Vendange Tardive

MURÉ, CLOS ST. LANDELIN, Rouffach
Négociant
Grand Cru Vorbourg (1985)   ②

Broad, spicy, buttery nose, earthy, rose-petal, spicy fruit on the palate, clumsy, broad, slightly buttery. Quite heavy, flat style. Medium term keeping. 5-8 years.
See also Vendange Tardive

DOMAINE OSTERTAG, Epfig
Propriétaire viticulteur
Generic (1985/87)   ① / ②

Spicy, light, floral, aromatic fruit, elegant, quite lightweight, with good length of elegant fruit, quite lean style. Medium term keeping. 3-6 years.

Nothalten (1986/87)   ②

Lean, delicately spicy fruit, quite restrained, less markedly varietal. Soft, floral fruit, quite dry, austere, with good length of flavour and good ageing potential. Medium term keeping. 4-8+ years.

Fronholtz (1984/86/87)   ② ★

Lovely soft, floral, smoky, peachy rosewater, with soft firm fruit and elegant tobacco, smoky spice. For long keeping, very restrained, well-balanced style. Keep 5-10 years.
See also Vendange Tardive

LÉON OSTHEIMER BOERSCH, Barr
Propriétaire viticulteur
nv   ②

Sweet, slightly spicy nose, perfumed, not very positive. Lightweight, spicy, soft fruit on the palate, not very varietal, a little thin, lacking in flavour. Unexciting.

CAVE VINICOLE DE PFAFFENHEIM, Pfaffenheim
Co-operative
Generic (1985)   ②

Light floral nose, roses, lychees. Rosewater fruit on the palate, with light restrained spice, a slight spritz and good varietal character. Fairly lean, with a little residual sugar. Medium weight, good classic style, drinking well in its youth, not for long keeping. 2-6 years.

PFLUGER-HAEGEL, Dambach-la-Ville
Propriétaire viticulteur
Generic (1986) ☑

> Soft, buttery nose, vanilla, hint of spice. Soft, light, spicy fruit on
> the palate, a little sappy, gentle, not very long flavour, pleasant,
> but without strong varietal character. Medium term keeping.
> 3-6 years.

VICTOR PREISS, CAVE VINICOLE BENNWIHR,
Bennwihr
Co-operative
An alias of the Cave Co-operative de Bennwihr.
Marckrain (1985)

> Fat, opulent, floral nose. Slightly baked, earthy, rich, spicy fruit
> on the palate, quite well-balanced, but not strongly varietal.
> Good length of flavour, quite attractive, but a little flat, blowsy.

PREISS ZIMMER, Riquewihr
Négociant
Generic (1986) ☑ ★

> Very perfumed, spicy nose, pommade. Very perfumed style on
> the palate, strong rosewater flavour, lean, elegant, with good
> varietal flavour and medium length. Well made classic
> Gewurztraminer of the 'perfumed' style. For young drinking.
> 2-5 years.

Réserve, Année Exceptionelle (1983) ☑ ★

> Very spicy nose, ripe, almost raisiny. Sweet, ripe, spicy fruit on

the palate, with the solid, ripe, raisiny style of the '83 vintage, and an almost 'late-picked' flavour. A little residual sugar. Good varietal flavour, good length. For medium term drinking. 5-8 years.

LES PRINCES DE TERROIR, Marlenheim
Négociant
Generic (1986) ☑ ★
Soft, fat, rosewater nose. Slight spritz, with rich, earthy, full-flavoured broad fruit on the palate. Quite powerful, spicy, weighty wine, with good varietal flavour. Medium length. Medium term keeping. 3-6 years.

VIN D'ALSACE
Appellation Alsace Contrôlée
LES PRINCES DU TERROIR
Gewurztraminer 70 cl
Mis en bouteille par LES PRINCES DU TERROIR à 67520 Alsace
PRODUCE OF FRANCE

JULIEN RIEFFEL, Mittelbergheim
Propriétaire viticulteur
Zotzenberg (1986) ☑ ★
Quite positive, spicy, rosewater nose. Soft, rich, lightweight fruit on the palate, slightly sappy, youthful, restrained, gentle fruit, clean, with good varietal character and well balanced medium length. Slight hint of residual sugar. Short to medium term keeping. 2-6 years.

ROLLY GASSMANN, Rorschwihr
Propriétaire viticulteur
Generic (1984) ☑
Honeyed, peachy nose. Attractive, light fruit on the palate, pleasant, but more characteristic of the vintage tasted than of the

grape, with quite high acidity and rather light body. Not a
success in this vintage.

SOCIÉTÉ VINICOLE STE. ODILE, Obernai
Co-operative
Clos Sainte Odile (1985)   2 / 3

Spicy nose, with hints of bananas. Gentle, rather sweet fruit on
the palate, some aromatic floral character, but not very
characteristic and rather sweet banana fruit. Rather strange,
atypical. Not recommended.

CHARLES SCHLERET, Turckheim
Propriétaire viticulteur
Generic (1985)   2 ★

Rich, fat, opulent nose, with hints of rose-petals, cloves, turkish
delight. Lovely rich, spicy fruit on the palate, cinnamon and
cloves, ripe, attractive, not overblown, with good individual
character, good weight and a very clean finish. Very well-made
wine. Short to medium term keeping. 3-6 years.

DOMAINE SCHLUMBERGER, Guebwiller
Propriétaire viticulteur
Princes Abbés (1938/85)   2

Soft, rosewater nose. Gentle, soft, rosewater spice on the palate,
with hints of grapefruit, quite floral, gentle, medium weight and

length, with good varietal character. Short to medium term keeping. 3-6 years.

Fleur de Guebwiller (1985) ②

Leaner, more floral style, rosewater, very perfumed spice. Quite lean, not heavy, with good length, and good varietal flavour. Short to medium term drinking. 3-6 years.

Grand Cru Kessler (1983/85) ③ ★

Soft, fat, spicy, broad style, beefy, grapefruity, blowsy style. Rich toasty fruit, powerful, full-blown, for lovers of big, rich Gewurztraminer. Big earthy fruit, which takes a few years to evolve. Medium term drinking. 4-8 years.

Grand Cru Kitterlé (1982/83/85) ④ ★★

More discreet style than the Kessler and potentially longer lived. Leaner fruit, still quite broad, but with more backbone, leaner, longer flavour. Still very rich, broad style, often very closed when young, taking 3-4 years for the nose to develop. Medium to long term drinking. 5-10+ years.

See also Vendange Tardive

RENÉ SCHMIDT, Riquewihr
Négociant

Cuvée Particulière, Réserve (1985)

Faint, sweet, spicy nose. A little sweet, dilute on the palate, quite alcoholic, but without richness. Lacking varietal character, a little uninteresting.

ROLAND SCHMITT, Bergbieten
Propriétaire viticulteur

Grand Cru Altenberg (1985)   2 ★

Soft, floral, spicy nose and palate, delicate flowery, aromatic style, without much weight, but with delicate varietal flavours and with good length. Very clean, well-made lightweight wine, for medium term drinking.

ALBERT SCHOECH, Ammerschwihr
Négociant

Generic (1985) ② ★

Soft, spicy, rosewater nose. Attractive, warm, rosewater spice on the palate, with a little residual sugar. Good length of tobacco spice fruit, well-balanced, medium weight, with good varietal flavour. Short to medium term drinking. 2-6 years.

MAURICE SCHOECH, Ammerschwihr
Propriétaire viticulteur

Generic (1985/86) ②

Soft, lightly spicy, rosewater nose and palate, medium weight, with a hint of residual sugar. Short to medium term drinking. 2-5 years.

Kaefferkopf (1985/86) ② ★

Until 1985, M. Schoech only had Gewurztraminer on the Kaefferkopf vineyard, and so did not bother to put the grape on the label. Now that he has planted Riesling as well, he uses the vineyard without the grape to denote his best Gewurztraminer. Quite full, spicy, ripe, rich fruit, with a hint of residual sugar. Fuller flavoured and richer than the generic, with more body. Short to medium term drinking. 2-7 years.

SCHROEDEL SARL (same firm as J. B. Adam and Veuve Joseph Pfister), Sigolsheim
Négociant

Florimont (1986) ②

Their réserve personelle cuvée. Soft, floral, turkish delight nose. Clean, light, spicy fruit on the palate, restrained, gentle, clean, with good varietal character, medium length and weight. Short to medium term drinking.

Réserve (1985) ②

Less positive nose. Clean, earthy, spicy fruit on the palate, attractive, medium length, elegant, with light spicy varietal character, and soft floral finish. Short to medium term drinking. See also Vendange Tardive

---

PAUL SCHWACH, Ribeauvillé
Propriétaire viticulteur

Sélection (1985) ②

Soft, spicy nose and palate, with gentle, ripe, raisiny fruit, lightly floral. Rather lacking in intensity, soft, without much varietal flavour and a little short. Not very exciting. Not recommended.

SICK DREYER, Ammerschwihr
Propriétaire viticulteur

Kaefferkopf (1983/84/85) ② ★

Very attractive, light, floral, cinnamon, rosewater fruit, with a slight hint of residual sugar. In '83 there was more than a hint, and this wine is almost late-harvest. The '84 and '85 were lighter, with gentle sweet spice, quite floral, delicate, with medium depth and length. Short to medium term drinking. 2-6 years.

SOCIÉTÉ VINICOLE À SIGOLSHEIM, Sigolsheim
Co-operative
Grand Cru Mamburg (1986) ☑ ★
Light, rose-petal, spicy nose. Lightweight, gentle, lean, spicy
fruit on the palate, herbaceous, medium weight, with very good
length. A wine that needs time to develop. Good varietal
character, well-made. Medium to long term drinking. 3-8 years.

J. SIPP, Ribeauvillé
Propriétaire viticulteur
Réserve (1985/86) ☑
Medium weight wine, floral, rose-petals, smoky, gently spicy.
Quite soft, full-blown style, with a little residual sugar.
Attractive, quite forward wine, without much backbone, good
varietal character. Short to medium term drinking. 2-6 years.
Réserve Personelle (1985) ☑ / ☒ ★
Made from old vines – 35 to 40 years old. Broader, more serious
style of wine, closed when young and with a fatter, more spicy,
firm fruit flavour. A little residual sugar, medium weight wine,
with good varietal character. Medium term drinking. 4-8 years.
See also Vendange Tardive

LOUIS SIPP, Ribeauvillé
Négociant
Generic (1985) ☑
Cedary, cigar-box nose, lychees, tobacco. Drier fruit on the
palate, herbal, lightly aromatic, lean. Rather unexpected, but

quite attractive. Medium length, not very varietal. Short to medium term drinking. 3-7 years.

Osterberg (1983) ☒ ★

Fatter, more earthy wine. Rich, soft, powerful, spicy, rosewater fruit, quite restrained, well structured, with good weight, and a long finish. Very well-made wine for medium to long term drinking. 5-8 years.

PIERRE SPARR & SES FILS, Sigolsheim

Négociant

Mambourg (1981/83) ☒ ★

Rich, powerful, ripe, earthy, rosewater spice, serious wine, richly aromatic, with hints of lychee, grapefruit. Well-structured wine, with full-flavoured fruit and slight residual sugar. Needs time to develop. Medium to long term drinking. 5-10+ years.

Brand (1983) ☒ / ☒

Quite gentle, ripe, raisiny fruit, almost late-picked in style. Restrained soft varietal flavour, with some residual sweetness. A little lacking in concentration. Sweet, pleasant, attractive, but a little dilute. Medium term drinking. 5-8 years.

See also Vendange Tardive

JEAN-BAPTISTE THOMANN, Ammerschwihr

Propriétaire viticulteur

Kaefferkopf (1985/86) ☒

Light, spicy fruit, floral, quite gentle, rather lightweight. A little lacking in character. Pleasant, but rather short, dull.

F. E. TRIMBACH, Ribeauvillé

Négociant

Generic (1983/85) ☒

Lightweight, gentle, rosewater, grapefruit, spice, soft, elegant. A little acidity to balance. Gentle varietal character. Short to medium term drinking. 2-5 years.

Réserve (1983/85) ☒ ★

A slightly more intense cuvée, at about another £1 a bottle. More weighty, dry, spicy, with more intense fruit and a little more power. Still quite restrained character. Worth the extra over the basic. Medium term drinking. 3-8+ years.

Cuvée des Seigneurs de Ribeaupierre ☒ ★★

The top cuvée, made from Trimbach's own vineyards. Always softer, riper, with more weight of fruit. Develops rich, smoky, apricot fruit with ageing. Broader, more peachy, spicy character, heavier weight. Quite closed when young and capable of very

long ageing. Medium to long term drinking. 5-10+ years.
See also Vendange Tardive

CAVE VINICOLE DE TURCKHEIM, Turckheim
Co-operative
Cave Tradition (1986) 1

> Discreetly perfumed, rosewater nose. Soft, gentle, lightweight
> spicy fruit on the palate, with good varietal character. Very
> clean, with medium weight and length. Good value. Short to
> medium term drinking. 2-5 years.

Grand Cru Brand (1983) 3

> Quite pungent, spicy nose and palate, full-bodied, solid, earthy,
> with quite aggressive spice. Rather lacking in charm. The weight
> and alcohol are there, but not the fruit. Acceptable, but
> disappointing. Medium term drinking. 5-7 years.

See also Vendange Tardive

MAISON WIEDERHIRN, Riquewihr
Propriétaire viticulteur
Réserve Personelle (1986) 3

> Floral, rosewater nose. Elegant, quite lightweight spicy fruit on
> the palate. Good varietal character, with excellent balance.
> Quite light restrained spice, delicate, but with good length.
> Well-made wine for early to medium term drinking.

ALSACE WILLM, Barr
Négociant
Generic (1985) 2

> Attractive, floral, spicy nose and palate, soft, gentle, with good

varietal character, and medium weight and length. Not heavily spicy, dry, well-balanced wine for early to medium term drinking. 2-5 years.

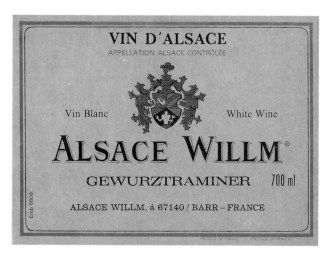

Cuvée Spéciale Emile Willm (1981/83)　③

This has one great advantage in that it is one of very few Alsace wines available in magnum. A late-picked wine, but without much late-picked character. Attractive, soft, spicy fruit, very pleasant, clean, but not a lot different from their basic cuvée.

Clos Gaensbroennel, Réserve Exceptionelle (1983)　③ ★

Willm's top cuvée, from their own vineyard. Rich, spicy, raisiny nose and palate, with fat, solid, buttery, ripe fruit and a very late harvest style. Some residual sugar, bags of ripe, intense fruit and

good varietal flavour. Quite high alcohol wine, which needs matching to food with care. Medium to long term drinking. 5-10 years.

See also Vendange Tardive

WOLFBERGER, Eguisheim
Co-operative
Generic (1986) ☐1

Light, floral, spicy nose, roses, wallflowers. Light, spicy, rosewater fruit on the palate, with a little residual sugar and an almost saccharine finish. Light gewurztraminer character, but a little cloying. For early drinking. 2-4 years.

DOMAINE ZIND HUMBRECHT, Wintzenheim
Propriétaire viticulteur
Generic (1985/86) ☐2

Soft, gently floral, spicy, slightly herbal/sappy when young. From vineyards in Wintzenheim and Gueberschwihr, some of which have very old vines. Develops meaty, spicy aromas with 2-3 years. Medium term drinking. 3-6 years.

Herrenweg (1985/86/87) ☐2 / ☐3 ★★

Achieves quite high degrees of oechsle even in cool vintages. Rich, almost oily, floral fruit, gentle, big, meaty style. Powerful, earthy, dry but intensely rich. Full-flavoured solid style which needs 2-3 years to develop its aromas. Medium term drinking. 3-8 years.

Heimbourg (1985/86/87) ☐2 / ☐3 ★★/★★★

From younger vines, grown in the calcareous soil at Turckheim. Peachy, soft, smoky, apricot, ripe fruit, less positively spicy and earthy, with ripe fruit aromas, grapefruit, apricots, peaches. Riper, softer fruit, still dry, but with great richness. Attractive in its youth, with medium term keeping potential. 3-7 years.

Goldert Grand Cru (1985/86/87) ☐3 ★★

From calcareous soil. More delicate, flowery, elegant spicy fruit, less heavy, more perfumed, lighter fruit. Still quite full-bodied, dry but rich, with a soft, more floral finish. Medium term drinking. 4-8 years.

Grand Cru Rangen (1983/85/86/87) ☐3 ★★

Rangen always has the strongest alcohol and reaches a very high oechsle, making Vendange Tardive quality in nearly every vintage. Even the 1984 achieved 110°. More peachy fruit, less spicy, with rich, fat, soft apricot fruit, smoky. Still dry, but very rich, soft and fat.

Grand Cru Hengst (1982/83/85) ☐3 ★

Always very spicy, ripe, gentle, quite forward. Fat, rich fruit,

lychees, ripe apricots, turkish delight. Broad, 'up front' wine, with masses of soft, spicy fruit and a warm, attractive spiciness. Less long-lived style, which drinks well in its youth. Short to medium term drinking. 3-8 years.
See also Vendange Tardive

GEWURZTRAMINER VENDANGE TARDIVE

JEAN BAPTISTE ADAM, Ammerschwihr
Négociant
Cuvée Jean Baptiste (1983) Vendange Tardive ③
Lovely honeyed, spicy nose, with a hint of spice. Not very varietal on the palate, but attractive, soft, medium sweet, with light grapefruit honeyed richness. Quite lightweight for Vendange Tardive, pleasant, without much concentration. Medium term drinking. 5-10 years.

DOMAINE LUCIEN ALBRECHT, Orschwihr
Propriétaire viticulteur
Vendange Tardive (1985) ④ ★★
Honeyed nose, spicy, ripe, slightly raisiny. Soft, spicy, smoky, honeyed fruit, medium dry, very rich, not much acidity, but with lovely long, gentle flavour. Well-balanced, with excellent depth of flavour. For long keeping. Long term drinking. 7-15+ years.

CAVE VINICOLE D'ANDLAU, Barr
Co-operative

Vendange Tardive (1985) ☐4

Very honeyed, almost mushroomy nose and palate, vegetal, spicy, honeyed, a little sugary/confectionery on the finish. Good length of flavour, but not very varietal. Medium sweet. Lacks the richness of botrytis. Medium term drinking. 5-10 years.

LÉON BEYER, Eugisheim
Négociant

Vendange Tardive (1983/85) ☐5 ★★

Grapes from the Eichberg vineyard. Gently spicy, with broad, powerful, rich fruit, strongly varietal. Ripe but quite dry. Broad, spicy elegance, not overblown. A much more 'food' style of wine, rich but dry, which would go well with foie gras, chicken in sauce. Very long flavour, which needs time to develop. Long term drinking. 8-20+ years.

Sélection de Grains Nobles (1983/71) ☐5 ★★★

The 1971 tasted recently was still very youthful and closed. This is a wine which needs years to develop. The 1983 had an oechsle of 165°. Both are surprisingly dry, with very rich, concentrated, intense, ripe, spicy fruit and discreetly rich sugar. The overall power and structure gives an impression of dryness and there is an excellent balance of acidity. Wines for very long term keeping. 10-30+ years.

PAUL BLANCK, DOMAINE DES COMTES DE LUPFEN, Kientzheim
Propriétaire viticulteur

Altenbourg Vendange Tardive (1983) ☐3

Ripe, spicy fruit, with broad, earthy, overblown roses perfume. Rich, off-dry, with big, fat, earthy alcohol weight. Big, full-blown style, immediately appealing, but with less backbone. Medium term drinking. 5-10 years.

Furstentum Sélection de Grains Nobles (1983) ☐5 ★

Very buttery, honeyed, botrytis nose. Rich, honeyed fruit on the palate, with good botrytis richness and elegant balancing acidity. Sweet and honeyed, excellent 'pudding' wine with good length of flavour. Medium to long term keeping. 7-15 years.

BOTT FRÈRES, Ribeauvillé
Propriétaire viticulteur

Réserve Personelle Vendange Tardive (1983) ☐4 ★★

Light floral nose, elderflowers. Soft, lighter weight fruit on the palate, quite lean, with elderflowers, roses, some spice and delicate varietal flavour. Medium dry, with some sweetness on the finish. Very individual style, not strongly varietal, but very attractive. Medium term drinking. 5-10 years.

ALBERT BOXLER, Niedermorschwihr
Propriétaire viticulteur
Vendange Tardive (1983)   4 ★★
Gently spicy nose and palate, soft, ripe, grapey, medium dry, with very ripe, gentle style. Soft, ripe, lychee fruit, medium length of flavour. Good varietal character. Medium term drinking. 5-10 years.
Grand Cru Brand Vendange Tardive (1985)   4 ★★
Spicy, rosewater nose and palate. Richer, more powerful fruit on the palate, quite astringent, almost stalky tannin. Powerful flavour, not much residual sugar, with good length of flavour. Firmer, bigger style. Medium to long term keeping. 8-20 years.

JOSEPH CATTIN, Voegtlinshoffen
Propriétaire viticulteur
Grand Cru Hatschbourg Vendange Tardive (1983)   3 ★
Soft, gently spicy nose and palate. Full-blown roses. Big, earthy, broad style, medium dry, very soft, with ripe, raisiny fruit. Very immediate appeal, not for long keeping. 4-8 years.

THÉO CATTIN, Voegtlinshoffen
Négociant
Grand Cru Hatschbourg Vendange Tardive (1985)   3
Rich, spicy, grapefruit nose. Perfumed, spicy, medium sweet

fruit on the palate, soft, lightly spicy, floral, with medium weight and length. No great concentration, but attractive, immediate style. Medium term drinking. 6-10 years.

DOMAINE MARCEL DEISS (Jean Michel Deiss), Bergheim
Propriétaire viticulteur
Grand Cru Altenberg de Bergheim Vendange Tardive (1985) ④ ★

Soft, spicy, raisiny, lychees nose. Rich, ripe, very spicy fruit on the palate, with good varietal character and rich, powerful, minerally, earthy fruit. Slightly herbal, restrained. Medium dry, with rich, round, soft fruit. Medium to long term drinking. 5-15 years.

DOPFF AU MOULIN, Riquewihr
Négociant
Grand Cru Brand Vendange Tardive (1981/83) ③ ★

Elegant, lightly spicy style, with rich, fat fruit and a hint of residual sugar. Lightweight, restrained style, with well balanced acidity. Gentle, elegant style for medium term drinking. 6-10 years.

Vendange Tardive (1985) ③

Still from the Brand vineyard, but Dopff have decided that it is confusing to label a wine both Grand Cru and Vendange Tardive, so from now on it is one or the other. Very discreet spice, off-dry, with good weight of fruit. Very closed and undeveloped at present, and hard to assess. Medium term drinking. 8-10+ years.

Grand Cru Sporen Vendange Tardive (1983) ③ ★★★

From a cold clay soil, giving less fatness. Lighter, fruitier style, with a cassis-like nose. Soft, very perfumed spicy fruit, patisserie spice, honey and flowers. Less powerful, more restrained. Lovely soft, ripe, blackcurrant fruit, off-dry. Very unusual attractive style, highly recommended. Short to medium term drinking. 5-10 years.

Sélection de Grains Nobles (1983) ⑤ ★★

Only 5,000 bottles produced, picked grape by grape on 24 November. 14·1° with 40 grams residual sugar. Very honeyed, powerful, grapefruit nose and palate, rich, floral, honeyed, very intense flavour, with lovely rich, raisiny fruit and very long finish. Very well-balanced, rich wine. Long term drinking.

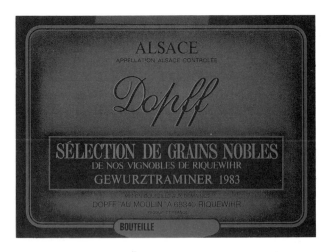

FALLER, DOMAINE WEINBACH, Kientzheim

Propriétaire viticulteur

Vendange Tardive (1985) ⑤ ★

Soft, rich, rose-petal, spicy nose. Rich, gentle fruit on the palate, medium dry, with balancing acidity and medium weight. Restrained, elegant style, with good varietal flavour. Medium to long term drinking. 6-10 years.

Sélection de Grains Nobles (1983) ⑤ ★★★

Faller made several selections in 1983, some of which are fantastically expensive, at around £50 a half-bottle. This is their less expensive selection at less than half the price. Picked at 124° oechsle, this wine has a rich, grapefruit, lychees nose, with powerful, concentrated fruit, licorice, rosewater, honey, with very clean, balancing acidity and superb length of flavour.

Lovely honeyed, elegant fruit, with superb balance. Medium to long term drinking. 8-20+ years.

JÉROME GESCHICKT, Ammerschwihr
Propriétaire viticulteur
Vendange Tardive (1983/85)   ③ ★★
Soft, peachy, raisiny, ripe fruit, big, earthy, spicy, quite broad, with some residual sugar and a gentle, broad, earthy style. Medium dry, but soft, smoky and peachy, with great richness. Medium length. Quite forward style. Medium term drinking. 5-10 years.

WILLY GISSELBRECHT, Dambach-la-Ville
Négociant
Vendange Tardive (1983)   ④ ★
Rich, honeyed, spicy fruit, powerful, bitter grapefruit flavour. Medium dry, with concentrated ripe, almost herbaceous gewurztraminer flavour. Medium to long term keeping. 8-15+ years.

HUGEL & FILS, Riquewihr
Négociant
Vendange Tardive (1976/83)   ⑤ ★
Always quite full-blown, earthy, rich style, with some residual sugar and a heavy, herbaceous, very perfumed flavour. Spicy, intense, ripe fruit, which needs several years to develop. Broad, solid style. Medium to long term keeping. 7-15 years.

Sélection de Grains Nobles (1976/83) ⑤ ★★
Very rich wines, the '76 had 130° oechsle, and the '83 156°. Very
honeyed, rich, fat, grapefruity wines, raisiny, powerful, with rich,
earthy spice. Medium sweet, not really 'pudding' wines and with
great ageing potential. Long term keeping. 15-30+ years.

ANDRÉ KIENTZLER, Ribeauvillé
Propriétaire viticulteur
Vendange Tardive (1983) ③ ★★
Very powerful, ripe, grapefruit-skin nose. Rich, full-flavoured
fruit on the palate, peachy, spicy, very ripe but not heavy.
Off-dry, with soft, ripe, honeyed fruit. Good foie gras wine.
Medium to long term drinking. 6-15+ years.

MARC KREYDENWEISS, Andlau
Propriétaire viticulteur
Kritt Vendange Tardive (1983/85/87) ③ / ④ ★★
The first vintage was in '83 and was fermented dry, giving a very
powerful wine with spicy, herbal, peachy overtones, almost more
Tokay than Gewurztraminer in character. The '85 and '87 have
some residual sugar and are medium-dry. Both retain the spicy,
herbaceous, smoky character and all are wines for long term
drinking. 8-15 years.
Sélection de Grains Nobles (1987) ⑤ ★★
Made for the first time in 1987. Very honeyed, powerful, rich,
raisiny fruit, with elegant balancing acidity, and the same
herbaceous, sappy flavour as his Vendange Tardive. Rich,
elegant, quite restrained fruit. Medium to long term drinking.
8-15 years.

KUENTZ-BAS, Husseren-les-Châteaux
Négociant
**Cuvée Caroline, Vendange Tardive Réserve Personelle
(1982)** ★
Soft, ripe, raisiny, grapefruit nose. Soft, lean, spicy fruit on the
palate, medium dry, quite lightweight for Vendange Tardive,
but with good length of flavour and nice balance. Well-made
attractive wine for medium term drinking. 5-10 years.

JÉROME LORENTZ, Berghiem
Négociant
Vendange Tardive (1983) ★★
Soft, spicy, raisiny, ripe nose and palate. Quite restrained style,

with good varietal character and some attractive raisiny, botrytis fruit. Medium dry, elegant, with very good length of flavour. Medium to long term drinking. 10-15+ years.

JULES MULLER, Bergheim
Négociant
Vendange Tardive (1983)   ④

Undeveloped, spicy nose. Gentle, quite sweet, soft, spicy fruit on the palate, herbal, tobacco fruit, gently spicy, medium sweet, quite elegant. A little soft and lightweight, but very attractive and appealing. Medium term drinking. 5-10 years.

MURÉ, CLOS ST. LANDELIN, Rouffach
Négociant
Vendange Tardive (1983)   ③ / ④

Quite big, broad, fat style, with high alcohol and soft, earthy fruit. Medium dry, quite blowsy, gently aromatic, faded roses, tobacco. For medium term drinking, without the balance for long keeping. 4-8 years.

Sélection de Grains Nobles (1983)   ⑤

Very rich, raisiny nose and palate, very botrytis style. High alcohol, quite broad, fat. Very rich, concentrated fruit, with a touch too much alcohol for perfect balance. Ripe grapefruit, peaches, fat earthy finish. Medium term keeping. 5-10 years.

DOMAINE OSTERTAG, Epfig
Propriétaire viticulteur
Vendange Tardive (1983/85) ★

The 1983 was fermented almost to dryness, with 14·8° alcohol and 10 grams of residual sugar. It is rich, dry, with soft, fat, peachy, smoky fruit and a lovely long, aromatic, complex finish. Rich, honeyed, but not overblown. Long term keeping. 10-15+ years. The '85 has more noticeable residual sugar and a sweeter, softer style, without botrytis. Medium to long term keeping. 5-10 years.

DOMAINE SCHLUMBERGER, Guebwiller
Propriétaire viticulteur
Cuvée Christine Schlumberger (1976/83/85)

Named after the grandmother of the current owner, Cuvée Christine is always made with about 115° oechsle. It has the classic heavy, rich, earthy fullness of their other wines, with rich, peachy smokiness, and good length of raisiny, spicy flavour. The 1985 probably has even better balance than the '83 or the '76 and will be wonderful in the mid-1990s. Medium to long term drinking. 10-15+ years.

Cuvée Anne Schlumberger (1976) ⑤ ★★★

Anne was Christine's first daughter. This wine is only made in exceptional vintages, and has sadly not appeared since 1976. Previous vintages were 1964, 1967, 1971. The '76 has a full, old gold colour, with a rich, honeyed, barley sugar nose, buttery, rich, concentrated, raisiny, with a very rich, syrupy, honeyed fruit and good balancing acidity. It is quite soft and is drinking very well now. Picked at 156° oechsle. Medium to long term keeping. 10-20+ years.

SCHROEDEL SARL (same firm as Veuve Joseph Pfister and J. B. Adam), Sigolsheim
Négociant
Vendanges Tardives (1985)   ③ ★
  Floral style, rosewater and glycerine. Off-dry, light, elegant, with good weight of flavour and light, spicy, ripe fruit. Quite lean, lightweight. Medium term keeping. 5-10 years.

JEAN SIPP, Ribeauvillé
Propriétaire viticulteur
Vendange Tardive (1983/85)   ③ ★
  The '83 was picked at about 112° oechsle, and the '85 at 115°. Both have a broad, soft, spicy, earthy fruit and a gentle, smoky, peachy, spicy flavour. Medium dry, not over heavy, with good, lean length of flavour. Good foie gras/munster wine. Medium term drinking. 5-10 years.

PIERRE SPARR & SES FILS, Sigolsheim
Négociant
Mambourg Cuvée Centenaire Vendange Tardive (1981/83) ☑ ★
Soft, perfumed, earthy richness of fruit, with quite high alcohol. Broad, soft, full-flavoured, earthy wines, medium sweet/medium dry, with rich, raisiny fruit and long finish. Very closed when young. Medium to long term drinking. 8-15+ years.
Mambourg, Cuvée Centenaire, Sélection de Grains Nobles (1985) ☑ ★
Rich, spicy, raisiny fruit on palate, quite intense, vegetal, herbaceous flavours, with very good length of flavour. No evidence of botrytis (there was little in 1985, although the neck label here states that the grapes are botrytis affected). Very attractive, rich, powerful fruit, which needs a long time to develop. Well-made, but expensive at around £25/£30 a half. For long keeping. 10-20 years.

F. E. TRIMBACH, Ribeauvillé
Négociant
Vendange Tardive (1976/83) ☑ ★
The '76 was broad, earthy and fat, the '83 a little leaner, with rich, smoky, spicy, rosewater, peachy fruit and a nice clean, grapefruity finish. Off-dry, with rich, ripe fruit which needs time to develop. Medium weight, quite restrained. Medium to long term drinking. 10-15+ years.

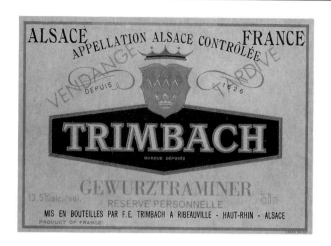

CAVE VINICOLE DE TURCKHEIM, Turckheim
Co-operative
Vendange Tardive (1983)   4 ★
Floral, spicy nose and palate, slightly bitter grapefruit, ripe
botrytis fruit, quite full-flavoured, concentrated, with good
length and weight of ripe fruit. Medium dry, quite serious wine,
with good structure. Good value at around £15. Medium to long
term drinking. 8-15+ years.

ALFRED WANTZ, Mittelbergheim
Propriétaire viticulteur
Grand Cru Zotzenberg Vendange Tardive (1985)   4 / 5
Soft, undeveloped, spicy nose and palate. Slightly mushroomy,
herbal, with gentle, ripe, soft, spicy fruit. Medium sweet, with a
little too much sugar for the body. Alcohol shows through a little.
Gentle medium weight wine. Medium term drinking. 3-6 years.

ALSACE WILLM, Barr
Négociant
Clos Gaensbroennel Vendange Tardive (1983)   4 ★★
Lovely rich, spicy, raisiny, honeyed, botrytis nose. Rich, raisiny,
grapefruit, spice on the palate, almost oily, butter, bitter ripe
grapefruit, with great concentration and plenty of botrytis
flavour. Medium dry, with very rich, intense ripe fruit. Spicy,
floral and very appealing. Long term drinking. 10-15+ years.

DOMAINE ZIND HUMBRECHT, Wintzenheim
Propriétaire viticulteur
Grand Cru Rangen Vendange Tardive (1985) ④ ★★
   Picked at 115° oechsle. Ripe, soft, spicy, rosewater fruit. Elegant,
   quite fat, with an elegant, rosewater fruit. Medium dry, with 15
   grams residual sugar. Very soft, ripe style. Medium term
   drinking. 5-10 years.
Grand Cru Goldert Vendange Tardive (1985) ④ ★★
   More perfumed, rosewater nose and palate, smoky, rich, elegant,
   with rich, fat, spicy fruit, but still quite delicate. Elegant, lighter
   weight style, medium dry. Medium to long term drinking.
   5-15 years.
Grand Cru Hengst Vendange Tardive (1976/86) ④ ★★★
   Rich, full flavoured, soft, gentle, spicy fruit, which develops
   smoky, buttery, peachy character with age. Off-dry, less raisiny,
   with very long, persistent flavour and excellent balance and
   backbone. More backward style, which needs longer ageing.
   Long term drinking. 10-20 years.

Heimbourg Vendange Tardive (1986) ④ ★★★
   After the grapes for their Sélection de Grains Nobles had been
   chosen in 1986, the rest were used for a Vendange Tardive.
   Honeyed nose, hints of botrytis, with rich fruit and a buttery,
   rich, elegant, ripe fruit, high glycerol, with a touch of new oak.
   (Aged for one year in small oak casks.) Unusual, rich, fat, ripe
   fruit, elegant, with great potential. Medium to long term
   keeping. 5-15+ years.

Herrenweg Vendange Tardive (1986) ④ ★★

Soft, rosewater nose, turkish delight, honeyed, botrytis. Medium dry, with rich, sweet, honeyed, ripe fruit. More forward style. Medium term drinking. 4-8 years.

Herrenweg Sélection de Grains Nobles (1986) ⑤ ★★★

The domaine made Sélection de Grains Nobles for the first time in 1986 and made four different cuvées (not all for commercial sale). The Herrenweg was picked at 130° oechsle, and has a rich, raisiny grapefruit nose, with rich, oily, honeyed fruit on the palate and lovely acid balance. Lovely long, intense flavour, with a hint of buttery oak (matured partly in new oak). Medium to long term drinking. 5-15+ years.

Heimbourg Sélection de Grains Nobles (1986) (n/a)★★★

Picked at 168° oechsle. Only 750 litres were produced and the grapes for this cuvée took twenty people one week to pick. Very intense, powerful, raisiny, botrytis fruit, buttery, honeyed and elegant, with very good balance of acidity. For long term keeping, if any were available!

Grand Cru Rangen Sélection de Grains Nobles (1986) (n/a)★★★

Only 650 litres of this wine were produced. More grapefruity, with very honeyed, botrytis fruit, less forward, more closed. Intense, ripe, botrytis fruit, with clean acidity and tremendous length. For long term keeping, if any were available!

MUSCAT

The Muscat grape has been grown in Alsace since the sixteenth century. It was often used to produce *vins de liqueur* and *vins de paille*, or *Strohweine*. These wines were once considered to be amongst the best sweet wines of France, but production was dying out by the late 1920s. The original vine type grown in Alsace was the Muscat Blanc à Petits Grains, also known as Muscat Canelli or Muscat de Frontignan. It is a type of wild Chasselas, said to have originated in ancient Greece. There is also a pink-skinned version: Muscat Rose à Petits Grains. It is very particular about the soil in which it is planted and has to be planted in vineyards offering the best exposure to the sun, as it is late ripening. It is subject to mildew and rot and to poor flower set. Generally Muscat produces good wines in three or four years out of ten. In the mid-nineteenth century, Muscat Ottonel was introduced to the region. It is also subject to rot, mildew and poor setting, but has the advantage of slightly earlier ripening. It has smaller, finer grapes and produces a more perfumed, elegant wine, whereas the Petits Grains, or Muscat d'Alsace, has larger grapes, with a greener, more grapey flavour and gives body and weight. Muscat d'Alsace gives a more 'immediate' nose, strongly perfumed, almost catty, but which does not last well. Ottonel gives a more discreet nose, which develops well with age. The best wines are made from a blend of the two, with Ottonel representing around 70 per cent of the plantation and Petits Grains the remaining 30 per cent. Muscat grapes are also very attractive to birds (and to humans), bringing further depredations to the harvest!

Muscat is always a dry wine in Alsace. It has the characteristic grapey nose of fresh Muscat grapes and can be intensely perfumed, almost catty, or elderflower-like. On some soil-types the bouquet is more spicy and can be similar to Gewurz-traminer, but without the weight. On the palate, Muscat produces a light, soft, dry wine, very delicate, without a very strong flavour. The best wines have a flavour of fresh muscatel grapes and a juicy, very clean, fresh flavour, without strong acid or alcohol. The best wines, made from a blend of the two varieties, may take two to three years from the vintage to develop their bouquet and will last for many years. Generally speaking, most Muscats are at their best between two and four years from the vintage, but the better balanced wines, from a vintage that was neither too hot nor too cold, can last for 15 or 20 years, still holding their very fresh, youthful, perfumed fruit. In lesser years, old Muscats tend to take on an oily, earthy nose and palate, vaguely reminiscent of Riesling but with less acidity.

Muscat wines are ideal as an aperitif, being light in alcohol. They are also excellent with asparagus, onion tart or melon. They are best served at the beginning of the meal, as any more powerful wines would tend to mask their delicate perfume.

Muscat can be Vendange Tardive, or even Sélection de Grains Nobles, but very seldom is. The delicate, perfumed, grapey flavour is lost with late picking and it is the least successful variety for late-picked wines.

MUSCAT

JEAN-BAPTISTE ADAM, Ammerschwihr
Négociant
1985 ☒

Light, grapey, soft fruit, gentle style, pleasant, but not very obvious. Light varietal flavour, for drinking young.

CAVE CO-OPÉRATIVE DE BEBLENHEIM – see **BARON DE HOEN**

GASTON BECK, Zellenberg

Négociant

1985 ☐2

>   Light, spicy nose, a little dull, not very varietal. Quite spicy, grapey fruit on palate, soft, broad, with grapey, muscat fruit on the finish. Correctly made, but not very exciting.

J. BECKER, Zellenberg

Négociant (the same firm as Gaston Beck above)

Grand Cru Froehn (1985)

>   Light, discreet, spicy nose. Fragrant, grapey fruit on the palate, well-balanced, with good, positive, fresh grapes, muscat flavour and very good length. Needs a little time in the glass to develop, a wine that could take 3 to 4 years bottle age.

LÉON BEYER, Ribeauvillé

Négociant

Usually makes two cuvées, basic and reserve. In poor years only the basic cuvée is produced.

1986 ☐1 / ☐2

>   Light, fresh, grapey nose and palate. Firm, young, grapey fruit, dry but with a gentle soft fruitiness. Not very long flavour, but clean and well-balanced.

Réserve (1986) ☐2 ★

>   More positive, elderflower, grapey nose and palate, fresh, very clean and much more strongly varietal. Gives the sensation of eating fresh muscat grapes. Well balanced, firm wine. Good classic varietal flavour.

PAUL BLANCK, DOMAINE DES COMTES DE LUPFEN, Kientzheim
Propriétaire viticulteur
1985 ☑

Rather oily, clumsy fruit, with little varietal flavour and rather flat, disappointing. Medium length of soft, rather anonymous fruit.

EMILE BOECKEL, Mittelbergheim
Négociant
Réserve (1985) ☑

Light, delicate, aromatic nose, not very positive. Clean, grapey, floral fruit on palate, pleasant, mild, well balanced. Quite low acidity. Medium length of flavour. Gentle, attractive style.

BOTT FRÈRES, Ribeauvillé
Propriétaire viticulteur
Réserve Personelle (1986) ☑ ★

Very fresh, grapey, muscat nose and palate, good positive flavour of fresh grapes. Well balanced, very clean, quite soft. Good varietal flavour.

JOSEPH CATTIN, Voegtlinshoffen
Propriétaire viticulteur
Grand Cru Hatschbourg (1985) ☒ / ☑ ★

Very rich, floral grapey style, almost aggressively muscat

perfume. Elderflowers, spicy fruit. Broad, fat, spicy, dry fruit, very long, fat flavour. Rich without being blowsy.

DOMAINE MARCEL DEISS (Jean-Michel Deiss), Bergheim
Propriétaire viticulteur
Cuvée Particulière (1985) ② ★
From grapes grown near Bergheim, on the Altenberg and Pflanzer vineyards. Light, restrained muscat nose. Fresh, youthful, very grapey flavour, quite soft, mild, with gentle varietal flavour. Well-made.

JEAN PIERRE DIRLER, Bergholtz
Propriétaire viticulteur
Grand Cru Saering (1985) ②
Not very varietal nose, a little 'cheesy'. Gentle, grapey fruit on the palate, lightweight, soft, a little short. Some good varietal flavour on the palate, but a little disappointing on the nose.
1986 ②
The 'plain' generic Muscat showed better than the Grand Cru. Maybe the Grand Cru was just a little young, but it did not seem to have the scope for development. The 1986 had a clean, fresh, light, minerally nose not strongly varietal, but fresh, lively and grapey. Very attractive.

DOPFF & IRION, Riquewihr
Négociant

Dopff & Irion make a generic Muscat and a single vineyard wine, Les Amandiers.

Les Amandiers (1983/85) ②

Both vintages of Les Amandiers show a pleasant, soft fruit, but neither were strongly varietal. Pleasant, grapey wine, the '85 more full-bodied, but both quite mild, soft. Even with 24 hours after opening, the bouquet does not develop much.

FALLER, DOMAINE WEINBACH, Kaysersberg
Propriétaire viticulteur

1986 ② ★

Attractive wine, with very floral, grapey nose and a strong, positive flavour of fresh grapes. Good length and intensity of clean fresh flavour. Classic varietal flavour, with a sensation of eating fresh grapes.

VICTOR GAERTNER, Ammerschwihr
Propriétaire viticulteur

1985 ② ★

Light, spicy, grapey nose. Surprisingly positive, grapey, spicy, muscat fruit on the palate, persistent. Good classic muscat flavour, very well-made.

JÉROME GESCHICKT, Ammerschwihr
Propriétaire viticulteur

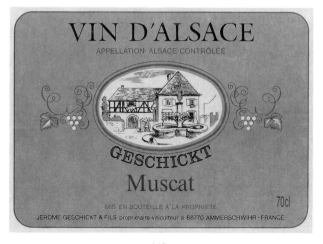

1986 2 ★

Positive, spicy, elderflower nose, floral, very attractive. Light, grapey, lean, catty fruit on the palate, with a good persistence of elderflower character. Leaner, drier style, quite sappy, less fruity. Will last well.

LOUIS GISSELBRECHT, Dambach-la-Ville
Négociant
Réserve (1985) 1 ★

Attractive, pungent, catty, elderflower nose and palate, lean style, medium weight, with spicy, grapey, muscat flavour. Well-made.

WILLY GISSELBRECHT, Dambach-la-Ville
Négociant
Réserve (1986) 1 / 2 ★

Light, delicate, floral nose and palate, softer, gentler, more delicate wine. Lovely fresh, grape flavour, very clean, medium length. Good aperitif wine, quite soft and mild.

JEAN HEYWANG, Heiligenstein
Propriétaire viticulteur
1986 2 ★

Soft, fragrant, gentle fruit on nose and palate. Light, fresh, grapey flavour, less pronounced on the palate than on the nose. Pleasant light style. Made mainly from Ottonel, with up to 20% Muscat d'Alsace.

BARON DE HOEN, Beblenheim
Co-operative
Cuvée Particulière (1985) 2 ★

Light, grapey fruit on nose and palate, with a clear flavour of fresh, ripe grapes. Straightforward, well-made wine, with good varietal flavour and good length. Very good aperitif wine.

MARCEL HUMBRECHT, Gueberschwihr
Propriétaire viticulteur
Marcel Humbrecht makes both a generic and a Grand Cru Goldert.
Grand Cru Goldert (1985) 2 ★

Floral, perfumed, muscat nose. Discreet, elegant, slightly spicy, grapey fruit on the palate, with more positive weight of alcohol. Seems to have a slight sweetness, with soft, spicy, almost gewurztraminer fruit. Lovely long, soft grapey finish. Very well-made.

JOSMEYER, Wintzenheim
Négociant
Josmeyer make a Réserve, and Les Fleurons, their top cuvée.
Réserve (1985) ②
Soft, grapey, muscat flavour, gentle, almost sweet, ripe fruit. Lightweight, gently aromatic, restrained style. Pleasant, maybe a little short.
Les Fleurons (1985) ②
This wine has a more minerally, spicy nose, with good muscat flavour on the palate, still quite lightweight, but well-balanced. Clean, fresh, grapey, with medium length.

VIN D'ALSACE JOSMEYER
APPELLATION ALSACE CONTROLÉE
Les Fleurons
Muscat d'Alsace
mis en bouteille par : JOS MEYER & FILS, A WINTZENHEIM HAUT-RHIN - ALSACE
PRODUCE OF FRANCE   e 70 cl
U.K. DISTRIBUTORS
HEDGES & BUTLER LIMITED - LONDON W.1.
WINE MERCHANTS SINCE 1667

ANDRÉ KIENTZLER, Ribeauvillé
Propriétaire viticulteur
Grand Cru Kirchberg de Ribeauvillé (1985/86) ② ★
This wine is made purely from Ottonel, and I have tasted several vintages. It often has an almost antiseptic/gentian nose when young, which develops to a spicy, grapefruity, grapey nose after 3 to 4 years. Light, spicy, almost sappy fruit on the palate, with good varietal flavour and the extra dimension of *terroir*. Not the usual, run-of-the-mill Muscat.

MARC KREYDENWEISS, Andlau
Propriétaire viticulteur
Clos Rebgarten (1985/6) ② ★

I have tasted several vintages of this wine which, despite its seeming air of delicacy, ages very well and retains its grapey, floral character. It is a very delicate, aromatic, direct style, lightweight and very gentle. After 2 to 3 years, it develops a peachy aromatic flavour, often with a slight lychee flavour. A good aperitif wine.

KUENTZ BAS, Husseren-les-Châteaux
Négociant
Réserve Particulière (1984) ②

A difficult vintage to judge Muscat. This wine had a soft, sweetish, almost raisiny nose, spicy, honeyed, attractive, but not recognisably Muscat. The varietal flavour was more evident on the palate, but the wine was a little oily, with quite high acidity and a little mean. A passable effort for the vintage.

FRÉDÉRIC MALLO, Hunawihr
Propriétaire viticulteur
1985 ②

M. Mallo makes his wine from 100% Muscat d'Alsace and aims to leave a suspicion of residual sugar. Grapey, fresh fruit on the nose and palate, slightly sappy, fresh, clean, medium weight, with good length of flavour. His wine needs at least 2 years to come round.

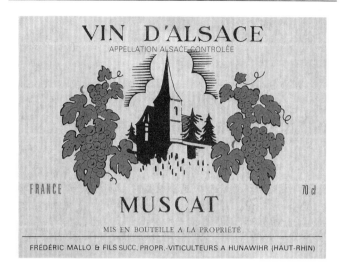

HUBERT METZ, Blienschwiller
Propriétaire viticulteur
1986 ②
Light, floral nose, not very positive. Clean, light, grapey fruit on palate, elegant, well balanced, fresh, delicate, well-made.

FRÉDÉRIC MOCHEL, Traenheim
Propriétaire viticulteur
Grand Cru Altenberg de Bergbieten (1985) ②
Very forward nose, floral, grapey and aromatic. Classic, grapey, muscat fruit on the palate, very clean, but with a slight astringency on the finish. Slight spritz. A wine for keeping 3 years from the vintage.

MURÉ, CLOS ST. LANDELIN, Rouffach
Négociant
Grand Cru Vorbourg (1985) ② / ③
In 1985 the Clos St. Landelin was upgraded to Grand Cru status. The 1985 Muscat had an almost spirity character, full-flavoured, earthy, but not very varietal. A hint of residual sugar and a discreet grapeyness. A little heavy-handed, characterless.

DOMAINE OSTERTAG, Epfig
Propriétaire viticulteur
1985/6 ② ★
I have tasted several vintages of this wine, which always has a

lovely fresh, grapey, appealing, aromatic nose. Light, fresh, quite gentle soft grape character on the palate, with good varietal flavour and good length. Well-made, keep 1 to 4 years from the vintage.

PFLUGER-HAEGEL, Dambach-la-Ville
Propriétaire viticulteur
1986 ②
　Pronounced grapey, elderflower nose, honeyed. Light, grapey

fruit on the palate, clean, not very positive, slightly buttery. A little short. Pleasant.

PREISS ZIMMER, Riquewihr
Négociant
1986/5 ☐2

Light, grapey, muscat flavour, gentle, a little lightweight. I found the 1986 rather lacking in character, with quite high acidity, whilst the 1985 had a warmer, more floral, fruit flavour. Generally a little dilute.

ROLLY GASSMANN, Rorschwihr
Propriétaire viticulteur
1983/4 ☐2 ★

The 1983 had a very attractive, flowery, muscat flavour, with the ripe, slightly oily richness of the vintage, but nevertheless a very clean, positive varietal flavour. The 1984 had the high acidity of the vintage, with a soft, honeyed fruit and less varietal flavour. Definitely a wine to follow, but avoid the poor vintages.

DOMAINE MARTIN SCHAETZEL, Ammerschwihr
Propriétaire viticulteur
1985 ☐2

Soft, earthy, spicy nose and palate, quite attractive, but not very varietal. Rich, spicy fruit on palate, with quite high alcohol and a rather soft, flat finish. Pleasant wine, but with little muscat flavour.

CHARLES SCHLERET, Turckheim
Propriétaire viticulteur
1986 ☐2 ★

Soft, ripe, fat, grapey fruit on nose and palate. Good varietal character, slightly off-dry and very quaffable. Medium length, clean, very well-made. Good aperitif wine.

DOMAINE SCHLUMBERGER, Guebwiller
Propriétaire viticulteur
1984/5 ☐2 ★★

Very positive, catty, floral, muscat nose and palate. Quite full-flavoured, with soft, quite fat, floral, muscat, grapey fruit and a nice sensation of freshly picked grapes. A very well-made wine, even in the 1984 vintage. Good, classic muscat of weightier style.

RENÉ SCHMIDT, Riquewihr
Négociant
Cuvée Particulière, Schoenenberg (1982)

Not a very good vintage to judge the wine by, but the one which was available on the UK market at the beginning of 1988. Soft, broad, spicy, floral nose. Gentle, soft, broad, earthy, grapey fruit on palate, with good balance of acidity, just starting to take on the oily, earthy flavours of age and with little varietal flavour. A pity, because the wine was probably very attractive 2 to 3 years ago.

ALBERT SCHOECH, Ammerschwihr
Négociant
1984 ☑

Honeyed, minerally nose, with slight oxidation. Clean fruit on the palate, with a little muscat flavour, but rather flat and dull. A shame to judge by this vintage.

SCHROEDEL SARL (same firm as Veuve Joseph Pfister and J. B. Adam), Sigolsheim
Négociant
Réserve (1986) ☑ ★

Clean, positive, floral, grapey nose, with fresh, youthful, grapey, muscat fruit on the palate. Soft, gentle, and very well balanced, with good varietal flavour. Very well-made.

PAUL SCHWACH, Ribeauvillé
Propriétaire viticulteur
1983/5 ☑

Quite positive, spicy, muscat fruit on nose and palate, the '83 developing an oily, petrolly fruit. Quite spicy, full flavoured, with good weight and length. Well-made.

PIERRE SPARR & SES FILS, Sigolsheim
Négociant
1985 ☑

Light, grapey, raisiny nose. Fresh, grapey fruit on the palate, mild, lightweight, pleasant, not strongly varietal. Medium length. Pleasant well-made wine, a little lacking in concentration.

JEAN-BAPTISTE THOMANN, Ammerschwihr
Propriétaire viticulteur
1986 ☑

We tried two bottles, both of which were rather woody, appley, with high acidity and little varietal flavour. Not recommended.

F. E. TRIMBACH, Ribeauvillé
Négociant
Trimbach make a Réserve quality, and in outstanding years, a

Réserve Exceptionelle, which can last an amazing length of time. The 1971 tried recently was superb, with very positive, rich, grapey, muscat fruit.

1984/85   ② ★★

Very attractive, intense, spicy muscat nose and palate. Even in 1984, this wine succeeded well and Trimbach made one of the best Muscats of the vintage. Always a good, classic style, never heavy, but with ripe, opulent highly reliable Muscat flavour in all vintages.

CAVE VINICOLE DE TURCKHEIM, Turckheim
Co-operative
1986   ② / ① ★★

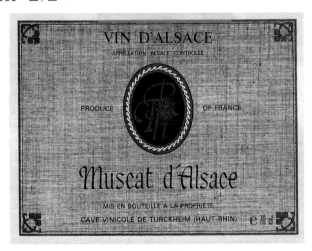

Lovely fresh, positive, grapey, muscat nose. Clean, fresh, soft, attractive grapey fruit on the palate, floral, classic, with good length of flavour. Very well-made wine, with strong varietal flavour. Excellent value.

MAISON WIEDERHIRN, Riquewihr
Propriétaire viticulteur
Réserve (1985) ②

Spicy, elderflower nose, but a touch 'cheesy'. Quite high acidity on the palate for the vintage, rather flat, dull and lacking in varietal flavour. Hints of muscat flavour, but no strong varietal character.

ALSACE WILLM, Barr
Négociant
1985 ②

Light, fresh nose, not very positive. Light, pleasant fruit on the palate, slightly aromatic, very soft, with little acidity. Quite pleasant, but a little neutral.

DOMAINE ZIND HUMBRECHT, Wintzenheim
Propriétaire viticulteur
The *Domaine* makes a straight Muscat and a Grand Cru Goldert. In poor vintages the wine is put into their Edelzwicker.
Generic (1985/86/87) ② ★

I have tasted several vintages of this wine, which is quite highly floral in character, with clean, very grapey fruit on the palate and quite lean, lightweight fruit. It is an attractive well-made wine, which improves with 2 to 4 years from the vintage.
Grand Cru Goldert (1986/87) ③ ★★★

Very powerful, minerally, grapey nose. Much more weight of fruit, with classic varietal character, and a powerful, minerally grapeyness. A wine which improves with 4 to 5 years in bottle. Very well-made, classic Muscat with several extra dimensions.

TOKAY-PINOT GRIS

The name Tokay-Pinot Gris causes some confusion: the grape variety, Pinot Gris, has been known as Tokay in Alsace since the mid-eighteenth century. Cuttings are said to have originally been brought to Alsace from Hungary by Baron Lazare de Schwendi in 1568, but the variety could just as easily have come from Burgundy since Pinot Gris is of the same family as Pinot Noir. Interestingly, cuttings were taken to Hungary from Burgundy in the fourteenth century, so could these be the variety later returned to France? Pinot Gris has always been highly regarded for quality in Alsace, although the quantity grown has always been quite small. About 681 hectares are now planted representing around 5 per cent of the total production of the region.

The grape was known as the Grauklevner in the seventeenth century and the Tokay from the mid-eighteenth century. Jullien distinguishes between Tokay and Tokay Gris in his *Topographie de Tous les Vignobles Connus*. It is the same variety that is known as Auvernat Gris, Pinot Beurot, Rulander and Malvoisie (although not the Malvoisie as in Malvasia or Malmsey). Today there are three clones grown: the Grand Moyen, which is not recommended, the Moyen Grain and the Petit Grain.

Tokay-Pinot Gris produces a wine that is high in alcohol, low in acidity, gently spicy, with a peachy, dried apricot, smoky, almost nutty flavour. Whilst less instantly appealing than the Gewurztraminer, Tokay is potentially the better wine and well-made examples can be very long lived. Tokay can be almost reminiscent of good white Burgundy and takes on a creamy, smoky, almost toasty aroma and flavour when mature. It is the ideal wine to partner foie gras and has sufficient weight to stand up to roast meats and game. In Alsace, it is the Tokay, rather than the red Pinot Noir, which would be served with game or with strongly flavoured meat dishes. Tokay is ideal with the local specialities baekeoffe or *choucroute*.

In good vintages, Tokay produces excellent Vendange Tardive wines. Like the Gewurztraminer, these wines have to be made from grapes reaching a natural must weight of 243 grams per litre, from which it can either be fermented dry or left with some residual sugar. Vendange Tardive Tokays are usually on the dry side, with most of the sugar turned into alcohol. Sélection de Grains Nobles can be wonderful and will repay long ageing.

As a general rule a basic Tokay will be at its best between two and five years from the vintage; a special reserve wine, a single vineyard or a Grand Cru wine will be at its best between five and fifteen years from the vintage; a Vendange Tardive wine between five and twenty years from the vintage; and a Sélection de Grains Nobles between eight and twenty years from the vintage. In particularly good vintages, Tokay will be the second longest-lived variety after the Riesling.

The EEC passed legislation in 1980 prohibiting the use of the word 'Tokay' for this variety, but since they somehow forgot to seek opinions or comments from Alsace the legislation has not been enforced and growers continue to label their wine variously: Tokay-Pinot Gris, Tokay d'Alsace or Pinot Gris, as the fancy takes them.

TOKAY-PINOT GRIS

JEAN-BAPTISTE ADAM, Ammerschwihr
Négociant
Cuvée Jean-Baptiste (1983)   ②
    Soft, rich, fat, spicy, peachy fruit. Gentle, forward style, with a
    soft, quite fat, rich flavour and medium length. Short to medium
    term drinking. 3-8 years.

DOMAINE LUCIEN ALBRECHT, Orschwihr
Propriétaire viticulteur
Grand Cru Pfingstberg (1985)   ③ ★
    Rich, fat, long, spicy style, peaches, dried apricots, very
    unctuous, with soft, rich, unctuous fruit. Good backbone, firm,
    with lovely length of ripe fruit. Very well-made. Medium term
    drinking. 4-10 years.

J. BECKER, Zellenberg
Négociant
Generic (1986)
    Light, soft, honeyed fruit, very gentle, mild, with just a hint of

peaches. Lightweight fruit, pleasant, but a little short. For
drinking young. 2-5 years.

LES VITICULTEURS RÉUNIS DE BENNWIHR ET ENVIRONS, Bennwihr
Co-operative
Réserve Marckrain (1985)
Light, dry fruit, quite earthy, but without much varietal
character. A little sulphury, lacking in character. Seems to have
quite a good weight of fruit, but it is hidden by sulphur.

LÉON BEYER, Eguisheim
Négociant
Generic (1985/86)   ②
Lovely clean, young, peachy fruit, spicy, fresh, medium weight,
dry, with good length of flavour. Very ripe, but not heavy.
Attractive well-made wine with good varietal flavour. Short to
medium term drinking. 3-8 years.
Réserve (1983/85)   ③ ★★
Made in good vintages, from grapes with a higher oechsle. This
cuvée is sometimes kept back in the best years for sale as Cuvée
Particulière. Broader, fatter style, more honeyed, flowery,
peachy, with a firmer, more weighty fruit. Very closed when
young, the Réserve needs at least 5-7 years and will last for
15-20 years.
See also Vendange Tardive

PAUL BLANCK, Kientzheim
Propriétaire viticulteur
Altenbourg (1985)   ②
Soft, ripe, peachy style, with a hint of residual sugar. Good
classic varietal flavour, with medium weight and length. Soft,
attractive wine. Short to medium term drinking. 3-8 years.

BOTT FRÈRES, Ribeauvillé
Propriétaire viticulteur
Réserve Exceptionelle (1986)   ③ ★
Soft, gently smoky fruit, medium weight, with a little residual
sugar. Gentle, attractive style, not a lot of backbone, but plenty
of ripe apricot flavour. Short to medium term drinking. 3-8 years.
Réserve Personelle (1985)   ③
Their top cuvée. A little richer, with soft, ripe, smoky, apricot
fruit and a little more residual sugar. Medium weight, quite

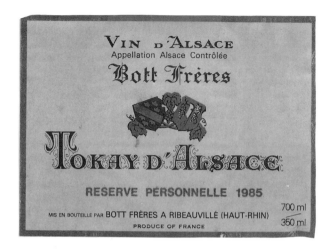

gentle, a little sweet for the amount of fruit. Medium term drinking. 4-8 years.

JOSEPH CATTIN, Voegtlinshoffen
Propriétaire viticulteur
Grand Cru Hatschbourg (1983/85)   ②/③ ★★
Broad, earthy, soft, peachy, ripe fruit, dry but very soft. Floral, fat richness, which develops quite rapidly. Soft, ripe, appealing style, with good varietal character. Short to medium term drinking. 3-8 years.

THÉO CATTIN, Voegtlinshoffen
Négociant
Grand Cru Hatschbourg (1985)   ③ ★
Very positive, smoky, honeyed, peachy nose and palate. Fat, earthy, off-dry, with rich, broad fruit. Firm, with good length and good varietal character. Short to medium term drinking. 4-8 years.

DOMAINE MARCEL DEISS, Bergheim
Propriétaire viticulteur
Bergheim (1986)   ② ★
Soft, peachy, smoky nose. Rich fruit on the palate, which needs time to develop. Good balance of acidity, soft, peachy, mellow and quite smoky, with medium length. Good varietal character. Medium term drinking. 4-10 years.

DOPFF AU MOULIN, Riquewihr
Négociant

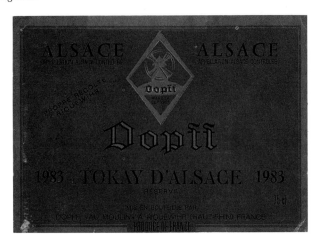

Tokay d'Alsace Réserve (1983)   2 / 3 ★
Made from their own vineyards. Firm, spicy, smoky wine, dry, with good weight of fruit and a firm flavour. Quite austere when young, needs time to develop. Classic, well-balanced, herbal, spicy wine, with good varietal character. Medium term drinking. 5-10 years.

DOPFF & IRION, Riquewihr
Négociant

Cristal de Pinot Gris (1982/83) ☐ / ☐
Light, soft fruit, rather anonymous, pleasant, but without much
varietal character. Ordinary quality commercial wine, for
drinking young.

Les Maquisards (1985)
Dopff's better cuvée. Richer fruit, peachy, quite fat, blowsy,
floral, earthy. Medium weight of fruit, quite good varietal
character. Ripe attractive fruit, medium weight. Medium term
drinking. 4-8 years.

FÉLIX EPPELÉ, Ammerschwihr
Propriétaire viticulteur
Generic (1985) ☐ / ☐
Soft smell and flavour of fermented apples. Gentle
banana/cooked apple fruit, with little varietal flavour. Not
recommended.

FALLER, DOMAINE WEINBACH, Kayserberg
Propriétaire viticulteur
Réserve (1983/84) ☐
Elegant, rich, soft, fat, peachy fruit. Leaner, more herbal style,
which is quite closed when young. Medium term drinking. 3-8
years.

Réserve Particulière (1985) ☐
Soft, smoky, rich fruit, honeyed, almost biscuity richness. Quite

firm style, which needs time to develop. Medium term drinking. 4-9 years.

Cuvée de la Sainte Catherine (1986)   ③ / ④ ★

Soft, rich, smoky fruit, more powerful aromas and taste, almost meaty, with rich, peachy, floral fruit. Heady, powerful, with very good length of flavour, which takes time to develop. Good varietal flavour. Medium term drinking. 5-10+ years.

VICTOR GAERTNER, Ammerschwihr

Propriétaire viticulteur

Generic (1986)   ② ★★

Soft, spicy, herbal, peachy, smoky nose. Rich, soft, gentle fruit on the palate, with good varietal character and good length of flavour. Gentle, soft style, dry but rich. Very well-made. Short to medium term drinking. 2-8 years.

JÉROME GESCHICKT, Ammerschwihr

Propriétaire viticulteur

Cuvée Reservée (1985)   ②

Soft, spicy, floral fruit, lightweight, lean, with pleasant, light spicy fruit. Gentle, less positive character and a little lacking in body, but clean and well-made. For drinking young. 2-5 years.

MAISON LOUIS GISSELBRECHT, Dambach-la-Ville

Négociant

Generic (1986)   ①

Soft, clean peachy nose, with pleasant, quite lightweight fruit on the palate. Lean, light, well balanced, with quite good varietal character. Lighter, less positive style, for drinking young. 2-6 years.

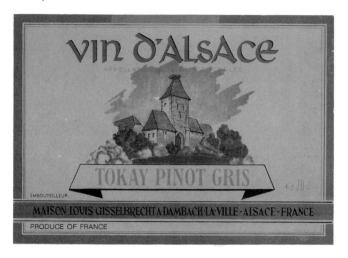

WILLY GISSELBRECHT, Dambach-la-Ville
Négociant
Médaille d'Or (1986) ☐1 ★
  Lovely floral nose, smoky, peachy, very positive. Rich, smoky, peachy fruit on the palate, well balanced, with good length of flavour. Medium weight, with good varietal character. Short to medium term drinking. 2-8 years.
See also Vendange Tardive

BARON DE HOEN, Beblenheim
Co-operative
Médaille d'Or (1985) ☐2
  Soft, smoky nose, almost oaky. Rich, spicy, full-flavoured fruit on the palate, soft, ripe, peachy. Medium weight and length, with very soft, light fruit and less pronounced varietal character. Pleasant wine for short term drinking. 2-5 years.

HUGEL & FILS, Riquewihr
Négociant
Generic (1985) Cuvée Tradition ☐2
  Soft, broad, floral fruit, gentle, quite soft and earthy, with medium length of flavour. Pleasant wine for short term drinking. 2-5 years.

Réserve Personelle ③ / ④ ★★

Much more powerful wine, rich, scented, peachy, with a lovely smoky intensity of flavour. Very spicy, broad, with good power. Very closed when young. Needs several years to develop. Classic varietal character. Medium to long term drinking. 5-20+ years.
See also Vendange Tardive

MARCEL HUMBRECHT, Gueberschwihr
Propriétaire viticulteur
Generic (1985) ②

Attractive light, floral, spicy nose and palate, quite honeyed, positive flavour, rich, dry, clean, with good varietal flavour. Quite perfumed style. Medium term drinking. 3-8 years.

ANDRÉ KIENTZLER, Ribeauvillé
Propriétaire viticulteur
Generic (1985/86) ② / ③ ★★

Quite vegetal, herbal style, with soft, rich, spicy, smoky nose and palate. Quite sappy/stalky when young, but with tremendous power and concentration of fruit. Lovely powerful, classic, varietal flavour. Long term drinking. 5-15+ years.
See also Vendange Tardive

KOEBERLÉ-KREYER, Rodern
Propriétaire viticulteur
Grand Cru Kloeckelberg (1983) ② ★

Light, soft, gentle, spicy fruit, elegant, quite lightweight, but

with very good length. Clean, light, floral spice, medium length of classic, light varietal flavour. Medium term keeping. 5-10 years.

CHARLES KOEHLY, Rodern
Propriétaire viticulteur
Grand Cru Gloeckelberg (1983) ☐2

Light, spicy fruit, gentle, quite lightweight, with a hint of residual sugar. Pleasant, a little too lightweight, but with nice gentle Tokay character. Medium term keeping. 5-8 years.

MARC KREYDENWEISS, Andlau
Propriétaire viticulteur
Lerchenberg (1986/87) ☐2

This is a new vineyard site since 1986, near Moenchberg. Leaner, minerally fruit, with slightly herbaceous sappiness. Aromatic, perfumed floral smoky fruit, with a hint of honey. Very lean, minerally style. Medium term keeping. 4-8 years.
Grand Cru Moenchberg (1984/86/87) ☐2 ★★

Made as a Vendange Tardive in 1985 and picked very late in '86 and '87. Soft, ripe, spicy fruit, with hints of ogen melon, peaches, apricots. Long, smoky, ripe, peachy nose and palate, which needs time to develop. Lovely exotic flavours, very individual, ripe without fatness. Very good clean length of flavour. Medium term drinking. 4-10 years, although older wines tasted have stood remarkably well up to 20 years.

See also Vendange Tardive

KUENTZ BAS, Husseren-les-Châteaux
Négociant
Cuvée Tradition (1985) ☐2

Light spicy fruit, quite gentle, soft, ripe flavour, less individual style, less varietal. Pleasant, lightweight wine without much individual character. Short term drinking. 3-6 years.

LANDMANN OSTHOLT, Soultzmatt
Propriétaire viticulteur
Bollenberg (1982) ☐2

Disappointingly flat, dull, with little varietal character. Soft fruit, a little peachiness, but rather cardboardy, sulphury. Not recommended.

FRÉDÉRIC MALLO, Hunawihr
Propriétaire viticulteur
Generic (1986) ☐2 ★★

Soft, 'tender' style, grown on a limestone clay soil. Spicy, flowery fruit, delicate, toasty, with a hint of honey. Good length of flavour, not heavy but very floral. The grapes reached 100° oechsle and the wine has 6 grams residual sugar. Short to medium term drinking. 3-8 years.

J. J. MULLER, Bergheim
Négociant
Cuvée Exceptionelle (1983) ☐2 ★

Soft, spicy nose and palate, buttery, smoky, peachy with round, soft, ripe, earthy, attractive fruit and good varietal flavours. Soft, gentle, ripe fruit, medium length and weight. Medium term drinking. 4-8 years.

MURÉ, CLOS ST. LANDELIN, Rouffach
Négociant
Clos St. Landelin (1981/83) ☐3

Soft, peachy fruit, quite gentle, lightweight. Good length of flavour, but without great depth. Pleasant, light fruit, clean, elegant. Medium term drinking. 4-8 years.
See also Vendange Tardive

DOMAINE OSTERTAG, Epfig
Propriétaire viticulteur
Barrique (1984/85/86/87) ☐3 ★★

André Ostertag is experimenting with oak fermentation and maturation for his Pinot Gris. The '84 was made a third in oak and is very attractive now, with the light acacia honey of the vintage. The '85 was a little too oaky on the palate, with strong, nutmeggy new oak and some lovely rich fruit underlying. In '86 he found the right balance; warm, honeyed new oak, rich, spicy, with lovely clean, ripe flavour and a hint of smoky spice. The wine goes through its malolactic fermentation and takes on a lovely buttery richness with age. The '87 looks set to follow in its footsteps, with clean, fresh, ripe fruit. 5-12 years.

Muenchberg (1987) ☐3 (estimated)★

1987 will be the first vintage for this wine, which has been vinified in 2-year-old *barriques*. Rich, ripe, smoky fruit, toffee and nuts, with a complex, rich, long, ripe fruit flavour. Well-balanced wine. Medium to long term drinking. 6-10+ years.

PFLUGER-HAEGEL, Dambach-la-Ville
Propriétaire viticulteur
Generic (1986) ☑

Soft, oaky, buttery, vanilla nose and palate, soft, spicy, quite buttery. Gentle, soft, peachy fruit, quite attractive, but without much varietal character. A little short on finish. Short term drinking. 2-5 years.

PREISS-ZIMMER, Riquewihr
Négociant
Generic (1985) ☐

Soft, gentle, peachy, spicy fruit, quite lightweight, lean, herbal. Clean but a little short. Quite good lightweight varietal character. Pleasant. Good value. Short to medium term drinking. 2-6 years.

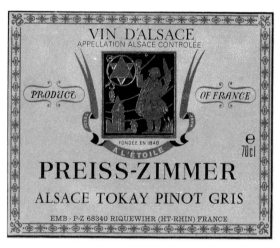

PIERRE RITZENTHALER, CELLIER DU MUHLBACH,
Ribeauvillé
Co-operative
Cuvée Réserve (1986) ☐ / ☑

Rather lightweight wine, with a hint of honey and spice, quite floral, gentle, but not very varietal. Pleasant flavour, but rather short, uninteresting. Short term drinking. 2-4 years.

ROLLY GASSMANN, Rorschwihr
Propriétaire viticulteur
Réserve Millésime (1984/85) ☑ ★

Attractive, soft, spicy fruit, even in the '84 vintage, when it was maybe a little too lean. Soft, mellow, ripe fruit flavours, lightly peachy, honeyed, with lovely balance of flavour, and good length. Medium term drinking. 4-8 years.

SOCIÉTÉ VINICOLE STE. ODILE, Obernai
Co-operative
Clos Sainte Odile (1985)   ② ★

The top cuvée from this co-operative. Soft, smoky, peachy, spicy nose and palate, with good varietal flavour. Quite rich, with soft, apricot fruit, well-balanced, with a hint of acidity and medium weight and length. Good straightforward classic Tokay flavour, very well-made wine. Medium term drinking. 4-8 years.

DOMAINE MARTIN SCHAETZEL, Ammerschwihr
Propriétaire viticulteur
Cuvée Réserve (1985)   ②

Quite rich fruit, earthy, full-flavoured, but rather over-whelmingly sulphury. Rich, spicy, soft, ripe fruit underlying, if the sulphur gets less obtrusive. At present quite hard to taste.

CHARLES SCHLERET, Turckheim
Propriétaire viticulteur
Generic (1985)   ② ★

Soft, gently spicy nose. Gentle apricots and peaches on the palate, very clean, with soft, smoky, elegant fruit, quite lean, with good power and length of flavour. Good varietal character.

Lovely balanced, rich wine, with undertones of fruits and spices. Very well-made. Medium term drinking. 3-10 years.

DOMAINE SCHLUMBERGER, Gueberschwihr
Propriétaire viticulteur
Réserve (1983/85) ③ ★
Lovely soft, smoky, rich fruit, very flowery, ripe, with a little residual sugar. Rich, quite heavy, with gentle, ripe, spicy fruit and a very ripe, almost sweet finish. Very closed when young, needs several years to develop. Medium term drinking. 5-10+ years.
Grand Cru Kitterlé (1985) ③ ★
The grapes from Kitterlé have always been put into the Réserve wine, and in 1985 for the first time a separate Grand Cru cuvée was made. Soft, peachy fruit, spicy, smoky, powerful, with a very minerally flavour and very good length of flavour. More restrained style, which needs several years ageing. Medium to long term drinking. 5-20 years.

MAURICE SCHOECH, Ammerschwihr
Propriétaire viticulteur
Generic (1985/86) ② ★/★★
In '85 this was almost a late-picked cuvée, with very honeyed, rich, smoky fruit and almost raisiny ripeness. The '86 is still fat and peachy, but a little lighter in weight. Gentle, smoky, with medium weight and length. Dry, but with a slight impression of

sweetness. A Vendange Tardive was made in '83, but not since. Short to medium term drinking. 3-8 years.

SCHROEDEL SARL (same firm as Veuve Joseph Pfister and J. B. Adam), Sigolsheim
Négociant
Generic (1986)   ☐1
Soft, attractive, ripe, smoky fruit, quite delicate style, well-balanced, rather lightweight, lean. Medium length, clean, with good varietal flavour. Good value. Short to medium term drinking.

PAUL SCHWACH, Ribeauvillé
Propriétaire viticulteur
Generic (1985)   ☐2
Quite positive nose, unusual aromas of almonds, bananas, and old champagne. Quite high spritz on the palate, with a strange, bitter almond finish. No varietal character, maybe a poor bottle. Not recommended.
Cuvée Selectionnée (1983)   ☐2
Stewed, cooking-apple nose. Honeyed fruit, appley, sweet and sour, with quite high acidity. Quite attractive in its way, with some spiciness and soft fruit. Much better palate than nose. Little varietal character. Short term drinking. 3-5 years.

SICK-DREYER, Ammerschwihr
Propriétaire viticulteur
Generic (1984/85)   ☐2
Soft, spicy, gentle style, quite forward, rich, with peachy aromas. Medium length of flavour, soft, peachy, light and elegant. Short to medium term drinking. 3-8 years.

JEAN SIPP, Ribeauvillé
Propriétaire viticulteur
Réserve (1986)   ☐2
Light, floral, peach nose. Clean, gentle, soft, spicy fruit, quite forward, easy drinking, with a hint of residual sweetness. Well-made, medium weight wine. Short to medium term drinking. 2-8 years.
Réserve Personelle (1985)   ☐2 ★
Picked at the beginning of November, for an almost Vendange Tardive style. Soft, spicy, peachy fruit, with hints of passion-fruit. Some residual sugar, gentle, soft, floral, not heavy.

Medium length of flavour, with good balance. Medium term drinking. 5-8+ years.

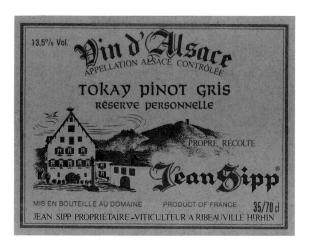

SOCIÉTÉ VINICOLE À SIGOLSHEIM, Sigolsheim
Co-operative
Generic (1985) ☐1 ★
Soft, honeyed, peachy fruit, with some residual sugar. Lightly spicy, smoky, with medium length. Good varietal character which needs time to develop. Medium term drinking. 4-8 years.

PIERRE SPARR & SES FILS, Sigolsheim
Négociant
Prestige, Tête de Cuvée (1985) ☐3
Spicy, smoky nose, with good weight of fruit. Ripe, firm, with good balance and length, still quite closed. Well-balanced wine with good varietal character. Medium term drinking. 5-8+ years.

F. E. TRIMBACH, Ribeauvillé
Négociant
Réserve (1983/85) ☐2 ★
Both vintages showed quite pronounced fruit in their youth, then retreated into their shell, needing several years more to come round. Very elegant fruit, restrained, with firm backbone, developing smoky flavours after 5 to 6 years. Medium term drinking. 5-15 years.

Réserve Personelle (1983)   4 ★★

Made in top vintages. Richer weight of fruit (about 92° oechsle, as against 80°ish for the Reserve). Very firm wine, with good weight of fruit, but very closed when young. Develops smoky, toasty, burgundian flavours with age. Long term keeping. 6-20+ years.

CAVE VINICOLE DE TURCKHEIM, Turckheim
Co-operative
Cave Tradition (1986)   1

Quite positive, smoky, peachy fruit on nose and palate, rich, quite fat, possibly a little too soft and fat. Gentle fruit, with medium length. Dry but a little lacking acidity. Pleasant. Short term drinking. 2-5 years.

MARCEL WEIBEL, Obernai
Propriétaire viticulteur
Generic (1986)   1 / 2

Lightweight fruit, gentle, soft, with light, peachy, smoky flavour. Well balanced, elegant, with medium length. Good varietal character. Short term drinking. 2-5 years.

MAISON WIEDERHIRN, Riquewihr
Propriétaire viticulteur
Generic (1986)   2

Leaner, lighter drier style, with more positive acidity. Light, floral spice, elegant, restrained, with medium weight and length. Pleasant, well balanced lightweight 'aperitif' style. Short to medium term drinking. 2-6 years.

WOLFBERGER, Eguisheim
Co-operative
Grand Cru Steingrubler (1985)   ③
> Quite positive, raisiny, late harvest nose. Ripe, positive fruit on
> the palate, ripe, fat, raisiny, spicy, with a little residual sugar.
> More earthy flavour, with the alcohol showing through.
> Develops rapidly, showing very mature flavours after 3 years.
> Good length of flavour, but a little clumsy. Short to medium term
> drinking. 2-6 years.

DOMAINE ZIND HUMBRECHT, Wintzenheim
Propriétaire viticulteur
Vieilles Vignes (1985/86)   ② ★
> Very rich, spicy smoky nose and palate, floral, peachy apricot
> fruit, with a little residual sugar. Gentle, quite spicy, with good
> varietal character, developing smoky, spicy, dried peaches
> flavour after 2 to 3 years. Short to medium term drinking. 3-8
> years.

Grand Cru Rangen (1985/86/87)   ③ ★★
> Firmer, drier style, with minerally, earthy flavour, almost
> herbaceous when young. Develops tones of quince, honey and
> spices. Very minerally, firm style, which needs long ageing.
> Medium to long term drinking. 5-15+ years.

See also Vendange Tardive

TOKAY-PINOT GRIS – VENDANGE TARDIVE

LÉON BEYER, Eguisheim
Négociant
Sélection de Grains Nobles (1983)   ⑤ ★★★
> Slightly spicy nose, with biscuity, smoky aromas. Medium sweet,

with good varietal character. Powerful, very long flavour, very complex. Wonderful balance of richness and flavour, almost a blend of a great Montrachet and Yquem. Needs long ageing. 10-30+ years.

Vendange Tardive (1983)   4 / 5 ★★

Soft, spicy nose and palate, with rich, dried apricot fruit and smoky richness of flavour. Restrained, rich but dry, with very good length of flavour. Long term drinking. 10-30 years.

ALBERT BOXLER, Niedermorschwihr
Propriétaire viticulteur
Grand Cru Brand (1985) Vendage Tardive   3 / 4 ★

Rich, powerful, herbal wine, quite sappy, firm, with broad, spicy fruit and ripe, intense flavour. Good varietal character, very closed. Medium to long term drinking. Needs 6-10 years minimum.

Vendange Tardive (1983)   4 ★

Softer, rosewater, spice, gentle, quite fat, with soft, fragrant, floral flavours, rich, ripe, peachy, voluptuous. Not a lot of acidity. Lovely gentle, ripe wine, with a little residual sugar and a great feeling of ripeness. Medium term drinking. 5-15 years.

DOPFF & IRION, Riquewihr
Négociant
Vendanges Tardives (1982)   3 / 4 ★★★

Attractive, spicy, almost grapefruit marmalade nose. Rich, spicy fruit on the palate, very peachy, smoky, honeyed. Hints of mushroom, undergrowth. Lovely long, complex fruit flavours, with very good balance. Medium dry. Medium term drinking. 6-15 years.

FALLER, DOMAINE WEINBACH, Kayserberg
Propriétaire viticulteur
Vendanges Tardives (1985) ④ ★
Very honeyed, rich, ripe fruit, quite blowsy style, with a little balancing acidity and good length of classic varietal flavour. Hints of wood smoke, peaches and raisins. Medium dry, with very rich raisiny fruit. Good balance of flavour. Medium term drinking. 4-15 years.

WILLY GISSELBRECHT, Dambach-la-Ville
Négociant
Vendange Tardive (1983) ④ ★★
Rich honeyed style, raisiny botrytis, with gentle spicy fruit. Medium sweet/medium dry, very honeyed, late harvest style, with good balance. Quite powerful fruit, earthy, rich, with very good length of flavour, needing time to develop. Medium term drinking. 8-15 years.

HUGEL & FILS, Riquewihr
Négociant
Vendange Tardive (1976/83) ⑤ ★
Rich, soft, broad, spicy, earthy fruit, medium dry, but with soft, broad richness of flavour, giving an impression of sweetness.

Broad, muscular style, which needs time to develop. Medium to long term keeping. 5-20+ years.

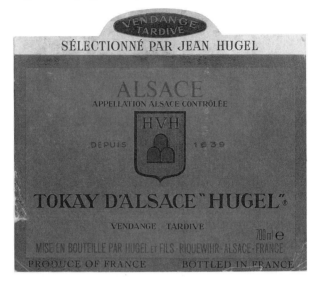

Sélection de Grains Nobles (1976/83) [5] ★★

Only a very small amount was produced in 1983, at an oechsle of 192° and this is being kept for the family. The '76 is just starting to develop well, with rich, ripe, raisiny fruit, honeyed smokiness and a big, broad, dried apricots and ripe melons flavour. Very scented, peachy, a wine for very long ageing. Long term drinking. 10-30+ years.

ANDRÉ KIENTZLER, Ribeauvillé
Propriétaire viticulteur
Sélection de Grains Nobles (1983) (n/a)★★

Sadly this wine is not for sale, as only 250 bottles were produced. Lovely rich, soft, ripe, peachy, smoky fruit, very concentrated, with rich, honeyed residual sugar and lovely intensity of ripe flavour. A wine which will last well into the next century.

MARC KREYDENWEISS, Andlau
Propriétaire viticulteur
Grand Cru Moenchberg Vendange Tardive (1985) [4] ★★★

Lovely gentle, smoky, buttery aromas, almost burgundian in character. Rich, intense, floral, biscuity fruit, some gentle residual sugar. Very strong varietal flavours, with the ripeness of late picking, but without botrytis. Very elegant, smoky wine, intensely long, with lovely balance and firm balance. Delicious now, but will last for many years. Medium to long term keeping. 4-15 years.

MUKÉ, CLOS ST. LANDELIN, Rouffach
Négociant
Vendange Tardive (1983) ③ / ④
Very soft, ripe, spicy, earthy fruit, quite raisiny, with high alcohol, and quite 'burnt' richness. Soft, broad, medium dry style, heavy, rich and earthy. Medium term drinking. 5-10 years.
Sélection de Grains Nobles (1983) ⑤
At first this wine seemed to have a very intense, botrytis, raisiny fruit, which changed after a few years to an almost dried raisin flavour. Now the wine is starting to develop a honeyed richness, with sweet, rich fruit. The alcohol is high and this is noticeable, giving the wine an impression of weight and almost of dryness. Big, earthy wine. Medium term drinking. 6-15 years.

DOMAINE ZIND HUMBRECHT, Wintzenheim
Propriétaire viticulteur
Vendange Tardive (1985) ④ ★★★
Picked at 110° oechsle, grown on the limestone soil of Rotenberg, next to Hengst. Very herbal, smoky nose, with rich, herbal, apricot fruit on the palate, ripe, powerful, off-dry, with very rich, ripe fruit flavour. Excellent varietal character, which needs time to evolve. Long term drinking. 6-20+ years.
Vendange Tardive (1983) Grand Cru Rangen ④ ★★★
Much more apricot flavour, raisiny, spicy, ripe fruits. Hints of peaches, quince, powerful, full-flavoured wine, with very little residual sugar. Long, intense, raisiny apricot finish. Long term drinking. 5-15 years.
Rotenberg Sélection de Grains Nobles (1986) (n/a)★★★★★
Only 400 litres of this wine were produced, picked at 150°-156° oechsle, giving a potential alcohol of 22°. Rich, smoky raisiny nose, with lovely raisiny botrytis fruit on the palate and wonderfully clean, balancing acidity. Very intense, buttery, rich, with a long, buttery finish.
Grand Cru Rangen Sélection de Grains Nobles (1986) (n/a)
★★★★★
A 'microvinification' of 25 litres. Powerful, smoky, raisiny fruit, intense, raisiny, botrytis flavours, honeyed, buttery, with very clean balancing acidity. Superb length of flavour. Heaven.

PINOT NOIR

Pinot Noir covers an area of around 870 hectares, representing 6·6 per cent of the total wine production. It was an important variety in the area in the Middle Ages, then lost popularity in favour of white varieties. Now it is again on the increase, although it is unlikely to attain much in excess of 7 to 8 per cent. The Pinot Noir is an old French variety, formerly known as Morillon, Noirien, Auvernat, Blauer Klevner or Schwarz Klevner. The word Pinot first appears in 1394, in letters addressed to Charles VI, and the word Pinot, Pineau or Pynos started to be applied to the vine. Guyot, writing in 1876, said that the reds of the Haut Rhin, representing one two-hundredth of the total production, were 'fine, light, delicate wines from the Gros Rouge and Pineaux Noirs'. He mentions as particularly good, and able to age well, wines from Ribeauvillé, St. Hippolyte and from Schlumberger at Guebwiller. At that time reds fetched high prices, about double the price of whites.

Pinot Noir is early ripening and has early budbreak, a factor which renders it sensitive to spring frosts. Cold weather at flowering can cause poor setting and subsequently small yields. The vine is quite delicate, with small clusters of grapes, the bunches often shaped somewhat like a pine cone. It is thought that the name Pinot derived from this fact. Pinot Noir grapes fetch the highest price of all Alsace grapes.

Over 90 per cent of Pinot Noir is vinified as rosé in Alsace, although there are some quite well-coloured reds. Guyot mentioned skin contact as being from two to six weeks, whereas nowadays it varies from three to four days, to a maximum of around two weeks. For the rosé wine, also known as Clairet or Schillerwein, Pinot Meunier may be added, although replanting vineyards with Pinot Meunier has not been permitted since 1975. The Pinot Noir grape does not have a very deep colour, and in the comparatively cool climate of Alsace, it is hard to attain more than a deep rosé to a light ruby. In spite of the lack of colour, it ages remarkably well, taking on a soft, brick red/brown tinge and developing a remarkably powerful bouquet. Pinot Noir can also be vinified as a white wine, away from the skins. It can then be used as a part (or total) of the blend for Klevner or Pinot Blanc. It can also be used in the blend for white Crémant, or on its own for Rosé Crémant. Often a wine labelled *rouge* will be quite pale in colour, even beside a wine labelled rosé. It is sometimes bottled in clear glass, so that consumers can see for themselves to avoid any confusion. Pinot Noir has only formed part of the Confrérie St. Étienne annual tasting since 1981.

Pinot Noir wines in Alsace have a light red colour, turning quite early on in life to a brick red. The bouquet is perfumed, reminiscent of raspberries, tinned strawberries and soft, ripe, sometimes slightly jammy, sweet fruit. The flavour is delicate, often slightly perfumed, with the characteristic earthiness of the region. It rarely has much, if any, tannin. Old Pinot Noirs, whilst not taking on any additional colour, nevertheless develop remarkably well, and take on the rich, vegetal, coffee flavours of a mature Burgundy. Pinot Noir is susceptible to noble rot, although this is to be avoided as it destroys the colour pigment. Occasional wines can be found that have had some noble rot, where the colour is almost tawny brown, but the bouquet and taste of these wines can be superb.

Although many growers are now using stainless steel and glass lined tanks for much of their vinification, Pinot Noir is almost always vinified in oak. It is the one variety in Alsace that has to undergo the malolactic fermentation, for the purposes of stability and flavour. Since the majority of producers in Alsace do not wish their white wines to undergo malolactic fermentation, Pinot Noir is usually vinified apart from the other wines, Many growers are experimenting with a more positive use of oak for Pinot Noir, using small oak casks rather than the large, old, traditional oval-shaped casks that were formerly in use. These wines, often designated *Vieilli en fût*, or *Barrique*, or *Fûts de Chêne* on the label, can be excellent, and often require longer ageing than the traditional wine. On occasions, however, the use of oak has been a little heavy-handed and the delicate Pinot flavour has been drowned in aggressive new oak flavour. In a very ripe vintage, such as 1983, the extra ripeness of the grapes was ideal for producing a wood-matured wine and examples such as Hugel's Réserve Personelle have all the power and structure of a fine Burgundy.

As a general rule, Pinot Noir wines are ready to drink as soon as they are bottled and are not intended for very long keeping. Wines from a light vintage will keep for up to four or five years, whilst wines from a good vintage may require keeping for two to three years from the vintage and will then last comfortably for eight to 10 years. Special cuvées may need ageing for four or five years and can last happily for 15 to 20 years.

Pinot Noir is usually served with charcuterie dishes, light meats and some cheeses. The lighter wines can be served lightly chilled.

PINOT NOIR

CAVE CO-OPÉRATIVE D'ANDLAU, Barr
Co-operative
Rouge d'Ottrott (1985)   ☐1 / ☐2

Pale rose colour. Soft, ripe, slightly jammy fruit on the palate, gentle, not very positive, ripe, very varietal, not very long. Well-made, classic, light Pinot.

J. BECKER, Zellenberg
Négociant
Rosé d'Alsace (1985)

Light red colour. Attractive, light, jammy fruit on the nose, with good weight of fruit on the palate, clean, soft, without much length of flavour but attractive.

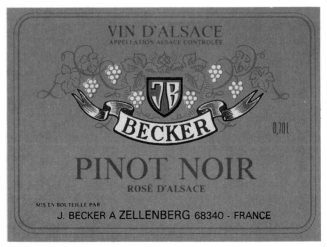

VITICULTEURS RÉUNIS DE BENNWIHR, Bennwihr
Co-operative
Fûts de Chêne (1985) ★
More pronounced colour than most, medium ruby. Soft, ripe fruit on the palate, with quite positive, oak flavour and a nice positive, ripe fruit finish. More structure than most, with good balance of fruit and oak. Needs keeping 4 to 5 years from vintage date.

LÉON BEYER, Ribeauvillé
Négociant
Léon Beyer makes a Rouge d'Alsace in all vintages, and a Réserve wine in top vintages, which will be released several years after the vintage.
Rouge d'Alsace (1983/5/6)   ①/② ★
I have tasted several vintages of this wine, which is always a light ruby colour, and made in the classic Alsace style. Very perfumed, light, fresh fruit, with little or no tannin. Made for drinking young, although it will keep for several years. Vinified for just 3 to 4 days on the skins and stalks.
Réserve   ④ ★★
This is a wine more likely to be found in the top restaurants than in shops. The 1971 tasted recently had an interesting, smoky, almost mushroomy flavour (there was some botrytis in this vintage). The nose was superb, with rich, mature, almost buttery fruit. An unusual wine, worth seeking out.

EMILE BOECKEL, Mittelbergheim

Négociant

1985 2

Light ruby colour. Very lightweight wine, classic Alsace style, but a little lacking in the delicious, raspberry fruit that this style needs. Pleasant, a little short.

BOTT FRÈRES, Ribeauvillé

Propriétaire viticulteur

Réserve (1985/86) 2 ★★

Bott Frères produce the classic, light ruby wine, matured in old oak. It is young, fruity and fresh, with a gently raspberry pinot flavour and almost a slight sweetness. Gentle and attractive. In exceptional years they keep some wine back for later release and a 1976 tasted recently was very interesting and unusual, with an almost late-harvest, raisiny fruit, like a dry, brambly blackberry/raspberry liqueur. Not typical of the variety, but worth trying.

THÉO CATTIN, Voegtlinshoffen

Négociant

Vieilli en Fûts de Chêne (1985) 2

Light rose-coloured wine, surprisingly light for a wood-matured style. Quite positive new oak on the nose and palate, with ripe, gently sweet, raspberry fruit. Very attractive, gentle, varietal flavour, but a little overpowered by oak.

DOMAINE MARCEL DEISS (Jean Michel Deiss), Bergheim
Propriétaire viticulteur
Burlenberg Vieilles Vignes (1985/86) ② ★

The cuvée from the old vines has one of the deepest colours for Alsace Pinot, with medium to full ruby hue. It is quite a positive, almost aggressive style of wine, which needs ageing for 5 to 10 years from the vintage. There is quite an oaky flavour underlying the fruit, which seems to give a slight bitterness/astringency when young and the fruit is rich, almost baked in flavour. I much preferred the 1985 to the 1986, which seemed to lack the same concentration.

Burlenberg (1985/86) ② ★

Medium ruby colour. A slightly lighter cuvée, from the younger vines of the same vineyard, with a very pleasing, smoky, raspberry fruit and a fresher, more immediate appeal. Still quite oaky, but with nice, round, ripe, jammy fruit and good length. This wine also needs time in bottle. Keep for 4 to 5 years from the vintage.

JÉROME GESCHICKT, Ammerschwihr
Propriétaire viticulteur
Cuvée Réservée (1985) ② ★

Light ruby colour. Made with quite a red wine feel, with good pinot noir character, a hint of tannin and a delicious raspberry/redcurrant fruit. Very attractive in its youth, but would also age well. Good classic Pinot, well vinified.

LOUIS GISSELBRECHT, Dambach-la-Ville
Négociant
Cuvée Réservée (1985/86)   ① / ② ★
   Light ruby colour. Soft, gentle, jammy, pinot fruit, very lightweight, but nevertheless red style rather than *rosé*, with quite good persistence of flavour. Good classic Alsace Pinot, for drinking young.

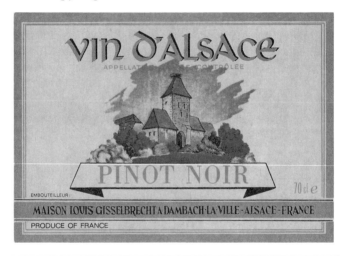

WILLY GISSELBRECHT, Dambach-la-Ville
Négociant
Réserve (1985/86)   ①
   Light tawny ruby, borderline between red and rosé. Light, gentle, soft, jammy fruit on the palate, with light, perfumed, pinot characteristics, but without much depth. Pleasant lightweight wine, a little lacking in substance.

HUGEL & FILS, Riquewihr
Négociant
Cuvée Traditional (1983/85/86)   ②
   Lightish ruby colour. Quite rich fruit on the palate, often with a little tannin when young, and with more 'guts' than many. More meaty style, definitely red rather than rosé, with quite positive style. This wine improves with 3-5 years from the vintage.

Réserve Personelle (1983/5) ③ ★★/★★★

Aged in second-hand barrels from Mouton Baron Philippe in 1982, and in new oak in 1983 and 1985. This wine is made in a Burgundian rather than an Alsace style, with a rich colour and powerful, chewy, ripe fruit, and a nice, nutmeggy oak. Very rich, long flavoured wine, which requires several years' ageing. Keep for 6-10 years from vintage date. Recommended.

RENÉ JOGGERST & FILS, Ribeauvillé
Propriétaire viticulteur
Cuvée Personelle (1985) Brandberg ①

Very pale ruby, more rose in colour. Sweet, slightly rubbery nose. Light sweetish rubbery fruit on the palate, short, unexciting. Not recommended.

MARC KREYDENWEISS, Andlau
Propriétaire viticulteur
Andlau Pinot Noir (1983/84/85/86/87) ① / ② ★

Generally light ruby colour, with soft, gentle, lightweight fruit on the palate. In some vintages there has been some oak ageing, and 1985 in particular was richer, more powerful, with a quite powerful raspberry pinot flavour. Keep 3-5 years from vintage.

KUENTZ-BAS, Husseren-les-Châteaux
Négociant
Réserve Personelle, Rouge d'Alsace (1983/85) ③ ★

Very good depth of colour. Ripe, herbaceous, pinot nose, almost Burgundian. A classic, rich pinot style, with some attractive new oak. A little astringent/bitter with wood tannin/wine tannin when young. Very good potential for long ageing. Needs keeping at least 7-10 years from vintage.

MICHEL LAUGEL, Marlenheim
Négociant
Rosé de Marlenheim (1981) ①

Deep rose colour. Soft, jammy, fruity nose and palate, pleasant, quite light, dry style, a little lacking in fruit, a little mean. Pleasant but rather light.

JEAN LUC MADER, Hunawihr
Propriétaire viticulteur
Cuvée Théophile (1985) ② ★

Lightish, tawny ruby. Sweetish, slightly vegetal nose. Light, sweetish, oaky fruit on the palate, lightweight, but with good varietal flavour and good length. A little oaky tannin. Attractive wine, but maybe a little heavy on the oak.

HUBERT METZ, Blienschwiller
Propriétaire viticulteur
1985/86 ☐ / ☑ ★★

Light ruby colour. Fresh youthful strawberry/raspberry pinot fruit. Traditional light style of wine, with just a hint of tannin, for drinking young. Medium weight of ripe fruit, good varietal flavour, classic light style.

MURÉ, CLOS ST. LANDELIN, Rouffach
Négociant
Vieilli en Pièces de Chêne (1983/85/86) ☐ ★

Light tawny ruby colour, except in '83, which was deeper. Soft ripe red fruits nose with a hint of new oak. Very rich style, with quite surprising amount of tannin when young and some oaky astringency. Very good length of flavour, with good potential for ageing. Needs 8-10 years from the vintage to soften out.

DOMAINE OSTERTAG, Epfig
Propriétaire viticulteur
1985/86/87 ☑ ★

André Ostertag is now maturing his Pinot in oak – some new,

some older – to give more complexity. Soft raspberry fruit,
medium weight. The '87 will be richer, with more toasty tannin.
Keep 3 to 5 years from vintage.

CHARLES SCHLERET, Turckheim
Propriétaire viticulteur
1984 ② ★

Light ruby, tawny colour. Positive, vegetal pinot fruit on nose
and palate. Gentle, strongly varietal, with soft, ripe fruit and
very little tannin. Well-made. Elegant style for drinking young,
2-4 years from vintage.

DOMAINE SCHLUMBERGER, Guebwiller
Propriétaire viticulteur
Pinot Noir (1985) ② ★

Light ruby colour. Fresh, raspberry, redcurrant nose and palate,
almost reminiscent of Cabernet Franc. Fresh, very clean fruit
flavour, without much tannin but with good length of flavour,
quite firm and good varietal character. Short to medium term
drinking. 3-8 years.

VIN D'ALSACE
DOMAINES SCHLUMBERGER

MARQUE DÉPOSÉE   PRODUCE OF FRANCE

e 700 ml

PINOT NOIR

APPELLATION ALSACE CONTRÔLÉE

MIS EN BOUTEILLE AUX DOMAINES SCHLUMBERGER
VITICULTEUR A GUEBWILLER (HAUT RHIN) FRANCE

ALBERT SCHOECH, Ammerschwihr
Négociant
1984 ★

Light, tawny ruby. Attractive, fresh, fruity, raspberry nose, with
clean, positive fresh varietal flavour. Soft, light fruit, with little

tannin. Classic light style for drinking young, 2-4 years from vintage.

MAURICE SCHOECH, Ammerschwihr
Propriétaire viticulteur
1985/86   ① / ②

Medium rose colour. Light fruit nose, not very positive. Clean, light, jammy, pinot fruit on the palate, attractive, fresh, very lightweight, more rosé style than red. Good aperitif style for drinking young.

PAUL SCHWACH, Ribeauvillé
Propriétaire viticulteur
1985   ①

Light, orange, tawny colour. Not very positive nose. Quite spritz on the palate, with light, herbal, sweetish fruit and a quite pungent, sweet spiciness with a little residual sugar. Different, not unpleasant, with nice, jammy pinot flavour.

LOUIS SIPP, Ribeauvillé
Négociant
1983   ① / ②

Pale rose, tawny colour. Sweet, soft, ripe, pinot fruit on nose and palate, with surprisingly positive, mature fruit on the palate. Soft and warm, with very attractive initial flavour, but which fades in the glass.

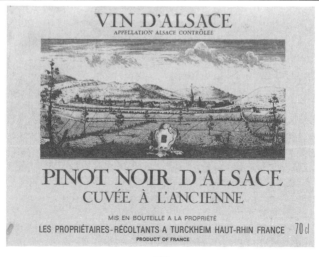

LES PROPRIÉTAIRES RÉCOLTANTS DE TURCKHEIM,
Turckheim
Co-operative
Cuvée à l'Ancienne (1983)　③ ★
Medium, brick, ruby colour. Ripe, powerful, jammy pinot noir fruit, with concentrated ripe cherry richness, and a hint of tannin. Quite powerful style, which needs several years from the vintage (5-7). Good potential for long ageing. More positive flavour than most.

ALFRED WANTZ, Mittelbergheim
Propriétaire viticulteur
Rouge de Mittelbergheim (1985)　② ★
Pale rose colour. Young, fresh, fruit nose, not very positive. Attractive young, jammy, raspberry fruit on the palate, soft, gentle, clean, not very long, but with good varietal flavour. Nice aperitif style. For drinking young (3-4 years).

MARCEL WEIBEL, Obernai
Propriétaire viticulteur
1985　①
Light ruby colour. Fresh, soft, jammy pinot nose and palate, lightweight, with no tannin and soft, gentle, raspberry fruit. Medium length, very gentle style. Pleasant, a little lacking in richness.

DOMAINE ZIND HUMBRECHT, Wintzenheim
Propriétaire viticulteur
1986/87 ② / ③ ★

Fermented in new Vosges oak, and aged for one year in oak. Medium ruby colour. Rich, ripe, raspberry fruit nose, with overtones of oak. Ripe pinot fruit on the palate, with a little tannin and quite positive oak flavour. Good varietal flavour, not heavy but well-balanced with very good length. Keep 4-5 years from vintage.

PINOT BLANC

The Klevner or Clevner grape was introduced into Alsace in 1742, and this wine has now become synonymous with Pinot Blanc. In fact the wine which can be sold under any of these three names can come from the Pinot Blanc, Auxerrois, Pinot Gris, Chardonnay, or Pinot Noir vinified as a white wine. Much of the production from Pinot Blanc and Auxerrois is also used in production of Crémant d'Alsace and in Edelzwicker. Pinot Blanc is considered to be a white mutation of Pinot Noir. It produces a rather hard wine, with high acidity. It has the potential to produce very good quality in a good year, but can often produce rather mean wine. The Auxerrois, also known as Pinot Auxerrois, although it is not in fact from this family, ripens earlier and produces a softer, spicier wine, with little acidity and higher alcohol. The Auxerrois is less productive than Pinot Blanc, but has high frost resistance. The Pinot Blanc is also known as the Morillon Blanc or Pinot Morillon. The strain used in Alsace is the Gros Pinot Blanc, giving a higher yield than in Burgundy. The Auxerrois, also known as Auxerrois de Laquenexy, is probably the variety originally called the Klevner.

Some producers vinify these two grapes separately, producing a Pinot Blanc and a second wine, labelled either Klevner or Auxerrois, but probably the best wines come from a blend of the two. Between them, they account for some 2,475 hectares of vines, producing around 21·8 per cent of the production. This is increasing, largely to the detriment of Sylvaner, as Pinot Blanc is considered to produce a more interesting wine. I have grouped all the wines labelled Clevner, Klevner, Pinot Blanc and Auxerrois under this one heading.

Pinot Blanc is generally light, fresh, dry, with moderate alcohol and clean acidity. The flavour should be fresh, sometimes lightly flowery or spicy, with soft, dry fruit. It is an uncomplicated wine, generally at its best from one to three years from the vintage. It is one of the least expensive wines of the region is becoming one of the best sellers on the UK market and is gaining in popularity in the United States. It works well on the richer soils of the plain and the area under vines increased rapidly in the 1970s.

Pinot Blanc is ideal as an aperitif, and is often served in *pichets*, as the carafe wine of the region. It can also be used as an inexpensive substitute for Riesling, with dishes such as *choucroute*, or with fish or white meats. When the blend contains some Auxerrois, the wine is often soft, with an almost peachy, fudge flavour and a slight spiciness which is very attractive.

PINOT BLANC/KLEVNER

CAVE VINICOLE DE BEBLENHEIM – see Baron de Hoen

GASTON BECK, Zellenberg
Négociant
Pinot Blanc (1986) ☐1
> Light, aromatic nose. Earthy, clean fruit on the palate, with a slight spritz. Well-balanced, fresh, with medium length. Pleasant, for drinking young.

J. BECKER (same firm as above), Zellenberg
Négociant
Pinot Blanc (1985) ☐1
> Light, aromatic nose and palate, earthy, soft fruit flavour, a little dull, lacking in ripeness.

LÉON BEYER, Eguisheim
Négociant
Pinot Blanc de Blanc (1985/86)　①

Clean, fresh, lightweight fruit, with good balancing acidity.
Flowery, not very long flavour. Quite lightweight, for drinking
young. Good aperitif style.

EMILE BOECKEL, Mittelbergheim
Négociant
Pinot Blanc Réserve (1986)　①

Faint nose. Light, pleasant fruit on the palate, clean, but without
much depth. Pleasant, fresh, rather short flavour, for drinking
young.

THÉO CATTIN, Voegtlinshoffen
Négociant
Cuvée de l'Ours Noir (1986)　② ★

Soft, fresh, floral nose. Soft, spicy, rich, dry fruit on the palate,
with an attractive almost fudge/butterscotch aftertaste. Rich,
gently dry, with a little soft acidity. Good length of flavour. Very
attractive unusual wine, with good individual character.

DOMAINE MARCEL DEISS (Jean Michel Deiss),
Bergheim
Propriétaire viticulteur
Pinot Blanc (1986)　②

Floral, quite spicy, honeyed nose and palate. Quite light, lean, with more noticeable acidity. Fresher, more herbal style, not much complexity, but very attractive. Good aperitif style, less fat.

DOMAINE EHRHART, Ammerschwihr
Négociant
Pinot Blanc (1986) ☐1

Fresh aromatic nose. Crisp, clean, light fruit on the palate, fresh, but rather anonymous, lacking strong character. Lightweight wine, pleasant, a little anonymous.

FALLER, DOMAINE WEINBACH, Kayserberg
Propriétaire viticulteur
Pinot Blanc (1986) ☐2 ★

Young, soft fruit nose. Very clean, floral, youthful fruit on the palate, fresh, well balanced, soft and mild, with good balancing acidity. Attractive, light fruit style, with good length of flavour. Well-made.

JÉROME GESCHICKT, Ammerschwihr
Propriétaire viticulteur
Pinot Blanc (n/v) ☐1 ★★

Soft, slightly peachy nose. Slight spritz on palate, with light, soft, spicy fruit. Gently ripe, slightly smoky, with light balancing acidity. Classic style, well-made.

LOUIS GISSELBRECHT, Dambach-la-Ville
Négociant
Cuvée Réservée (1985) 1️⃣

> Not much nose. Sappy, stalky, young fruit on the palate, slightly astringent, herbaceous, with slight bitterness on the finish. Quite lean, dry style, medium length. Pleasant.

WILLY GISSELBRECHT, Dambach-la-Ville
Négociant
Réserve (1986) 1️⃣ ★

> Slightly smoky, spicy nose. Clean, gentle, soft floral fruit, well-balanced, rich, peachy, with medium length and soft balance. Well-made mild style, very attractive.

Médaille d'Or (1986) 1️⃣ ★

> Slightly more positive, smoky, spicy nose. Rich, peachy fruit on the palate, a little fuller flavoured, with good length and balance. Peachy, elegant, soft and mellow.

E. HERING, Barr
Propriétaire viticulteur

Pinot Blanc (1985) 1️⃣ ★

> Soft, flowery nose, slightly spicy, not very positive. Soft, quite round, fat fruit on the palate, peachy, rounded, with a little acidity to balance. Quite short flavour, but well-balanced, with good varietal flavour.

BARON DE HOEN, Beblenheim
Co-operative
Pinot Blanc (1986) ☐1☐
Light fruit, slightly spicy, fresh, but somewhat lacking in character. A little short, dull.

VIN D'ALSACE
APPELLATION ALSACE CONTROLÉE

Baron de Hoen
Pinot Blanc

MIS EN BOUTEILLE A LA PROPRIÉTÉ

CAVES DE HOEN.VITICULTEURS REUNIS AU CHATEAU DE BEBLENHEIM.HAUT· RHIN .FRANCE

70 cl

Pinot Blanc (n/v) ☐1☐
Soft, peachy nose and palate, seemingly more attractive than the above. Clean, gentle, round, with a little balancing acidity. Soft earthy dry wine, easy drinking, with a light spritz.

HUGEL & FILS, Riquewihr
Négociant
Pinot Blanc de Blanc (also labelled Cuvée les Amours, or Les Vignards) ☐1☐ / ☐2☐
Soft, gentle fruit, often with a hint of spritz; sappy, herbal, dry, quite full flavoured. A positive style, earthy, dry, with medium length. More solid style.

MARCEL HUMBRECHT, Gueberschwihr
Propriétaire viticulteur
Pinot Blanc (1985) ☐1☐ ★
Very spicy, floral, aromatic nose, almost muscat/elderflower. Grapey fruit on the palate, peachy, soft, without much acidity. Slightly vegetal, herbal, sappy. Attractive, quite individual style, with plenty of flavour.

CAVE CO-OPÉRATIVE D'INGERSHEIM, Ingersheim
Co-operative
Pinot Blanc (n/v)   ①

> Warm, peachy earthy nose and palate, gentle, soft, with a little balancing acidity. Pleasant, lightweight, a little neutral.

JOSMEYER, Wintzenheim
Négociant
Cuvée du Printemps (1986)   ① ★

> Light, peachy nose. Light, clean fruit on the palate, with good balancing acidity. Attractive, floral, quite soft, with medium length. Good aperitif style.

Pinot Auxerrois Les Lutins (1983)

> The de luxe cuvée. Earthy, spicy nose. Clean, light fruit on the palate, floral but quite fat, rich. A little residual sugar. Bigger, broader softer style of wine. Well-made. From their own vineyards.

ANDRÉ KIENTZLER, Ribeauvillé
Propriétaire viticulteur
(1983/84/86) Auxerrois   ① / ② ★★

> Made purely from Auxerrois with no Pinot Blanc. In 1984 he experimented, vinifying the wine in oak. This gave a light, lemony oak fruit with the herbal acidity of the vintage, the fruit still showing well through the oaky flavour. In other vintages,

without the oak, the wine has a soft, floral, mellow ripeness, peachy, gentle, spicy, with hints of fresh brioche. It is a wine of quite high natural alcohol (13° in 1986), with very positive, auxerrois, peachy flavour. Unusually, a wine which will improve with 2-4 years ageing.

KUENTZ-BAS, Husseren les Châteaux
Négociant
Cuvée Tradition, Pinot Blanc (1986)
Quite earthy, weighty nose and palate, with a slight spritz and a hint of spice. Dry, but quite full flavoured, solid style. Well-made.

MARC KREYDENWEISS, Andlau
Propriétaire viticulteur
Kritt Klevner (1985/86) ② ★★

The wine sold under the Klevner label is purely from the Auxerrois, which is late-picked to give a smoky, peachy, spicy, late-harvest style, often with a little residual sugar. Hints of bitter orange, apricots, very floral, ripe and soft, with a little clean balancing acidity. In vintages when the Auxerrois is not ripe and distinctive enough, it is blended with the Pinot Blanc and sold under the latter name. The Klevner improves with 2-4 years ageing.

Kritt Pinot Blanc (1986/87) ① ★

This can be purely Pinot Blanc in a vintage where the Auxerrois has been vinified separately (1986), or it can be a blend of the two in a lighter year. Crisp, dry, fresh and clean, with a light herbaceous fruit. Lighter and drier, with more acidity. A fresh light aperitif wine, very clean.

JÉROME LORENTZ, Bergheim
Négociant
L'Ami des Crustaces, Pinot Blanc de Blanc (n/v) ①

Made, as the name suggests, to accompany seafood, this wine is light, crisp and fresh, with firm balancing acidity. The flavour is less positive than many and the finish somewhat short, but the wine is pleasant, although with a slight hint of sulphur.

JULES MULLER, Bergheim
Négociant
La Dame au Faucon Pinot Blanc (1985) ☐1

Attractive, floral, peachy nose. Firmer fruit on the palate, with good acidity and more attack. Slight spritz, rich, earthy, spicy fruit, drier, leaner style, with good length and balance. Well-made.

DOMAINE OSTERTAG, Epfig
Propriétaire viticulteur
Pinot Blanc (1984/86) ☐1 ★

Here also they have experimented with some oak ageing for Pinot Blanc. This cuvée without the oak is fresh, crisp, quite lightweight, with attractive, clean, light fruit, dry, with good balancing acidity. Attractive aperitif style, well-made.

Pinot Blanc 'Barrique' (1986) ☐2 ★

The oak-aged wine has a soft, buttery, oaky nose and palate, with gentle, restrained oak characteristics and a good weight of flavour. This wine is less typical of Pinot Blanc, but is a very attractive, interesting, different style, well worth trying.

JULIEN RIEFFEL, Mittelbergheim
Propriétaire viticulteur
Klevner Vieilles Vignes (1985) ☐1 ★★

Catty, spicy nose, green gooseberries, very fresh. Clean, light,

spicy fruit on the palate, very lightweight, with nice balance of acidity. Dry, fresh, very spicy, light style, with plenty of individual character. Recommended. Made from 100% Auxerrois.

ROLLY GASSMANN, Rorschwihr
Propriétaire viticulteur

Auxerrois Moenchreben (1986) ☐2 ★★

Soft, peachy, spicy nose and palate, fresh, clean, very well
balanced, quite soft, but with sufficient acidity to balance. Very
attractive, ripe, spicy style, medium length, with plenty of
Auxerrois character. Well-made.

DOMAINE MARTIN SCHAETZEL, Ammerschwihr
Propriétaire viticulteur
Pinot Blanc Cuvée Réserve (1985) ☐2

Quite positive, spicy nose, but with cheesy overtones, which
continue on the palate. Light, dry, with quite good fruit, but
marred by sulphury cheesiness. Disappointing.

DOMAINE SCHLUMBERGER, Guebwiller
Propriétaire viticulteur
Pinot Blanc (1986) ★★

Made from 50% Pinot Blanc and 50% Auxerrois, this wine has a
soft, floral, peachy nose, with rich fruit on the palate, quite soft
and mild, with a light balancing acidity and a little residual
sugar. Very gentle, cleanly-made wine, a little more weighty
than most.

RENÉ SCHMIDT, Riquewihr
Négociant
Pinot Blanc Réserve (1985)

Aromatic nose. Soft, warm, gentle, earthy fruit on the palate, a
little balancing acidity. Pleasant, very lightweight, but without
much individual character. Light aperitif style.

ALBERT SCHOECH, Ammerschwihr
Négociant
Pinot Blanc (1984) ☐1

Very much in the character of the '84 vintage, soft, honeyed,
mature, with hints of oxidation. Some gentle fruit remains, but
the wine is now rather flat, tired. Wait for the next vintage to
re-assess.

SCHROEDEL SARL (same firm as Veuve Joseph Pfister and
J. B. Adam), Sigolsheim
Négociant
Pinot Blanc (1986) ☐1

Light, fresh fruit nose and palate, quite earthy, pleasant, a little

short, but clean, dry. Good balance, a little lacking fruit flavour.
Pleasant aperitif style.

PAUL SCHWACH, Ribeauvillé
Propriétaire viticulteur
Pinot Blanc Réserve (1985) ②

Light, floral nose and palate, appley, young fruit, drier, with
firmer acidity. Fresh, clean, rather short flavour, pleasant, but
without much depth. Aperitif style.

SICK-DREYER, Ammerschwihr
Propriétaire viticulteur
Clevner (1982/83) ①

Soft, gently aromatic nose and palate, spicy, clean, elegant, with
good length. Dry but quite soft and round, a little fatter in style.

F. E. TRIMBACH, Ribeauvillé
Négociant
Pinot Blanc (1983/85) ① / ② ★

Very fresh, light, aromatic nose and palate, floral, crisp, quite
lean, with good balancing acidity. Firmer, drier style, slightly
herbal when young, with good length of flavour. Good aperitif or
fish wine.
Pinot Blanc Sélection (1983) ② ★★

In good vintages a better cuvée is made, which has weightier
fruit, still very dry and with firm acidity. Nice, crisp, floral,
herbal fruit, which takes 2-4 years to develop and lasts up to
6-8 years.

CAVE VINICOLE DE TURCKHEIM, Turckheim
Co-operative
Cave Tradition Pinot Blanc (1986) 1 ★

Soft, floral, peachy nose. Soft, gently spicy fruit on the palate, very well-balanced, with light acidity and attractive youthful fruit. Good length of flavour. Very well-made. Good value.

DOMAINE ZIND HUMBRECHT, Wintzenheim
Propriétaire viticulteur
Pinot Blanc (1984/85/86/87) 1 / 2 ★★

A blend of 50% Pinot Blanc and 50% Auxerrois. The Auxerrois usually undergoes malolactic fermentation, to give a softer, rounder, more buttery style (but not in 1987). Soft, rich, quite spicy, perfumed fruit, gentle, flowery, but with a very firm backbone and good length of ripe fruit flavour. A wine with lots of character, which improves with 3-4 years and can be kept 6-8 years.

SYLVANER

The Sylvaner grape, known in Hungary as the Cilifanthi, in Switzerland as the Johannisberg and in Germany as the Oesterreicher or Grunling, has been recorded in the Alsace region since 1870. It probably originated in central Europe, but another theory is that it is descended from a wild grape growing beside the Rhine. It is a very reliable producer in all weather conditions, giving consistently high yields, the highest average yield of all Alsace varieties, and for this reason it has always been quite widely planted. It is also resistant to rot. The main plantation areas are in the Bas Rhin, and between Westhalten and Thann in the Haut Rhin. When grown on flatter plain land it gives large yields of very neutral wine, but on a good site it can give a very attractive wine, especially in hotter vintages such as 1983. Sadly, one of its better sites, the vineyard of Zotzenberg in Mittelbergheim, has been classified Grand Cru and is therefore uprooting the Sylvaner vines in flavour of Grand Cru varieties. At present it is still allowed to be grown under the name Zotzenberg (without the Grand Cru), but this will probably be discontinued in the near future. The area currently planted with Sylvaner is 2,492 hectares, representing some 20·4 per cent of the production, but this is decreasing, mainly in favour of Pinot Blanc.

Although a late-ripening grape, it is generally picked early in the season to retain freshness and acidity. Fresh Sylvaner grapes taste almost like Sauvignon, with a very clean, ripe, herbaceous, gooseberry flavour, but the finished wine, whilst clean and fresh, does not have any very strong character and can indeed be extremely neutral. Sylvaner is relatively low in alcohol and high in acidity and can therefore, like Pinot Blanc, be used as an inexpensive Riesling substitute. It has a very fresh flavour, and makes an ideal aperitif wine, often being served locally by the *pichet*, or flagon. It is best when youthful and is not intended for long ageing, when it will lose its freshness and become rather dull and flat. It is generally one of the least expensive Alsace wines.

SYLVANER

JEAN BAPTISTE ADAM, Ammerschwihr
Négociant
Generic (1985)   ① ★
Attractive, fresh style, with almost minty, flowery nose and palate. Lightweight, fresh, clean and grapey. Light, fresh, aromatic style. Well-made.

DOMAINE LUCIEN ALBRECHT, Orschwihr
Propriétaire viticulteur
Generic (1985)   ① ★
Positive, aromatic, spicy nose, with a hint of elderflowers. Floral, delicate yet positive flavour, very fresh, with good length.

CAVE CO-OPÉRATIVE D'ANDLAU, Barr
Co-operative
Zotzenberg, Réserve du Président (1985)   ①
Soft, light style, with less acidity than many and gentle, floral fruit. Mild style, clean, lightweight, fresh and floral. No strong flavour, but pleasant.
Cuvée Divinal (n/v)   ①
Lighter, clean, crisp style, light acidity to balance, fresh but a little anonymous. Pleasant, but a little dilute. Better nose than palate.

LÉON BEYER, Eguisheim
Négociant
Generic (1985)
Soft fruit, a little acidity, a little more weighty, than most Sylvaner, earthy. Not much individual character.

JEAN PIERRE DIRLER, Bergholtz
Propriétaire viticulteur
Cuvée Vieilles Vignes (1985)   ② ★★
Peachy nose, almost late harvest style. Rich, dry fruit on the palate, good balancing acidity. Warm, earthy, with good length of flavour and a peachy, banana flavour. Less typical, but very attractive wine with plenty of character.

FALLER, DOMAINE WEINBACH, Kayserberg
Propriétaire viticulteur
Réserve (1985/86)   ② ★★
Intensely floral, aromatic, fresh nose. Crisp, clean, light fruit on

the palate, with slight spritz and almost a hint of residual sugar. Quite spicy, with plenty of character. Good classic varietal style.

VICTOR GAERTNER, Ammerschwihr
Propriétaire viticulteur
Generic (1985) 1️⃣

Soft, spicy, floral fruit on nose and palate. Gentle, ripe style, with light acidity to balance. Pleasant, attractive, but a little short and with no great personality.

JÉROME GESCHICKT, Ammerschwihr
Propriétaire viticulteur
Generic (n/v) 1️⃣ ★

Attractive, floral, spicy nose. Lightweight fruit, clean, pleasant, well-balanced, but with less character than on the nose.

ARMAND GILG, Mittelbergheim
Propriétaire viticulteur
Zotzenberg (1986) 1️⃣ ★

Soft, slightly peachy nose. Clean, light, herbal fruit on the palate, minerally, fresh, very clean, lean flavour. Purer, lighter style, with good classic varietal character and medium length. Well-made.

LOUIS GISSELBRECHT, Dambach-la-Ville
Négociant
Generic (1985) 1️⃣

Soft, spicy, attractive nose. Full weight on palate, earthy, slightly

sappy fruit. Slight astringency. A little hard, green. Medium
length of flavour. Solid style, lacking charm.

WILLY GISSELBRECHT, Dambach-la-Ville
Négociant
Médaille d'Or (1986) ☐
Faint nose. Clean, quite solid earthy, fruit on the palate, soft,
sound, a little low in acidity. Pleasant, unexciting.

J. HERING, Barr
Propriétaire viticulteur
Clos de la Folie Marco (1985) ☐ ★
Fragrant, floral nose. Quite fresh, light, minerally style, soft,
grapey, with attractive, crisp, clean finish. Good quaffing wine,
with classic varietal flavour.

JEAN HEYWANG, Heiligenstein
Propriétaire viticulteur
Generic (1986) ☐ ★
Soft, flowery, fruit nose, quite perfumed. Good weight of fruit,
quite full-flavoured, soft, ripe, well balanced. More powerful
style than many, with good individual character.

HUGEL & FILS, Riquewihr
Négociant
Generic (1985) ☐ ★
Clean, light fruit, a little fuller flavoured than many. Flowery,

spicy nose and palate, heavy fat style, fuller bodied than most Sylvaners. A good food wine, more robust, with less noticeable acidity.

CAVE CO-OPÉRATIVE D'INGERSHEIM, Ingersheim
Co-opérative
Generic (n/v) ☐1

Soft, floral nose, a little heavy, earthy. Flat, earthy fruit, solid, rather dull, clumsy. Quite short finish, and rather characterless.

MARC KREYDENWEISS, Andlau
Propriétaire viticulteur
Kritt (1985/86/87) ☐1 / ☐2 ★

Unusually, this is aged in Vosges oak for up to 6 months in some vintages. Quite smoky, oaky nose and palate, with the softness of ripe grapes and light acidity to balance. Slight hints of pears, peaches, with good length of flavour. Very attractive oaky wine, but without varietal character. In years without oak ageing the wine is crisp and fresh, and more typical.

GÉRARD LANDMANN, Nothalten
Propriétaire viticulteur
Generic (1985/86) ☐1

Both vintages had quite noticeable sulphur. Good weight of fruit, but a little hard, soapy, clumsy. Lacking in character and elegance.

FRÉDÉRIC MALLO, Hunawihr
Propriétaire viticulteur
Generic (1985/86) ☐1 ★

Lightly spicy, honeyed nose. Fresh, grapey, quite soft, with a little residual sugar. Gentle, clean style, with a little balancing acidity, but with more softness and less crispness than many. Very attractive.

DOMAINE OSTERTAG, Epfig
Propriétaire viticulteur
Generic (1985/86) ☐1 / ☐2 ★

Crisp, firm, sappy style, very clean, herbal. Uncomplicated fruit, quite floral, with good length of flavour. Classic varietal style. Good, lightweight, quaffing wine.

PFLUGER-HAEGEL, Dambach-la-Ville
Propriétaire viticulteur
Generic (1985) ☐1

Light, fresh, floral, lemony nose and palate, soft, lightweight, clean, quite delicate style. Not much power, but fresh, well-balanced and attractive. Light aperitif wine.

JULIEN RIEFFEL, Mittelbergheim
Propriétaire viticulteur
Zotzenberg (1986) ☐1 ★

Soft, floral, aromatic fruit, quite rich style, herbaceous, sappy, with good balancing acidity. Longer flavour, more positive. Attractive wine with plenty of character.

Réserve Zotzenberg (1986) ☐1 / ☐2 ★

Similar style, very clean, floral, herbaceous, with crisp, fresh acidity to balance and a little more weight and length of flavour. Unusually, a wine which will improve with a year or two in bottle.

DOMAINE MARTIN SCHAETZEL, Ammerschwihr
Propriétaire viticulteur
Generic (1985) ☐1 ★

Soft, peachy, fat style, slightly spicy, with quite weighty, earthy fruit. Good balancing acidity. A little more solid, with plenty of character. Recommended.

DOMAINE SCHLUMBERGER, Guebwiller
Propriétaire viticulteur
Generic (1983/85) ☐

Soft, floral fruit, spicy. Quite fat, weighty fruit on the palate, floral, quite earthy, with good balancing acidity. Medium length of flavour. More solid style.

SCHROEDEL SARL (same firm as Veuve Joseph Pfister and J. B. Adam), Sigolsheim
Négociant
Generic (1986) ☐ ★

Clean, earthy fruit, quite full-flavoured, positive, with a little acidity to balance. Good length of flavour, clean, well-balanced.

ALSACE SELTZ, Mittelbergheim
Négociant
Zotzenberg (1983) ☐ ★

Very perfumed, spicy nose and palate. Quite powerful, earthy, minerally, with good length of flavour and light balancing acidity. More character than many, with full-flavoured, rich, almost spicy fruit.

EMILE SELTZ, Mittelbergheim
Propriétaire viticulteur
Zotzenberg (1985) ☐

I tasted two bottles of this wine, both of which had a woody, casky, musty nose and palate. Rather musty flavour, not recommended.

F. E. TRIMBACH, Ribeauvillé
Négociant
Generic (1984/85) ☐ ★

Soft, perfumed nose, with a hint of spice. Light, fresh, refreshing flavour, with good balancing acidity. Slightly vegetal. Good, classic, varietal character, medium length. Clean, well-made, lighter, drier style.

ALFRED WANTZ, Mittelbergheim
Propriétaire viticulteur
Zotzenberg (1985/86) ☐

Lighter, leaner style, floral, quite herbal, with light acidity. Delicate fruit, a little bland, soft, with shortish finish. Quite attractive, light aperitif style.

CHASSELAS

The Chasselas, or Gutedel, accounted for over 20 per cent of the plantations at the beginning of this century, although Dr Jules Guyot, in the mid-nineteenth century, described the wine from Chasselas as 'detestable'. It was first grown in Alsace at the end of the eighteenth century and is said to have originated in the Loire valley, where it is still grown, producing such wines as Pouilly-sur-Loire. It is the same variety as the Fendant of Switzerland, where it produces attractive, light, fruit wines. There are many clones of this vine, which is distantly related to the Muscat family. It is quite early ripening, of irregular productivity and produces good dessert grapes. It is mainly used for the production of Edelzwicker, although a few growers bottle the wine separately. Nowadays only 291 hectares are planted with Chasselas, which accounts for about 2·6 per cent of the total production.

Chasselas produces a light-bodied wine, with low acidity and a soft, fresh flavour, not strongly distinctive. It is best drunk between one and four years from the vintage and is excellent as an aperitif or with light fish dishes.

CHASSELAS

HUGEL & FILS, Riquewihr
Négociant
Flambeau d'Alsace (n/v) ☐1☐
> Light, crisp, fruity wine, with a light earthiness. Clean, pleasant, with good balancing acidity. A good aperitif wine, without much individuality.

ANDRÉ KIENTZLER, Ribeauvillé
Propriétaire viticulteur
Chasselas (1984/85/86) ☐1☐ ★
> Light, fresh, youthful fruit, clean, lightweight, with a light spiciness. Very fresh, young aperitif wine, with an attractive, clean, young fruit flavour. Well-made.

SICK-DREYER, Ammerschwihr
Propriétaire viticulteur
Côtes d'Ammerschwihr PMG (1983/85)   ☐ ★

Young, fresh, lightly aromatic nose and palate, with soft, spicy fruit on the palate and clean, balancing acidity. Medium length. Attractive light aperitif wine. PMG stands for *pour ma gueule*, 'for my gob'!

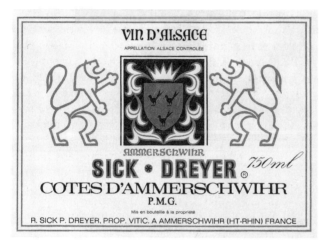

KLEVENER DE HEILIGENSTEIN

Klevener de Heiligenstein is a very localised Appellation, applying to some 15 to 20 hectares of Savagnin Rose, a clone related to the old Gewurztraminer vines of the region. The vine was introduced to the village by Ehrhardt Wantz, via Chiavenna in northern Italy and was formerly known as the Kleber or Klawer. Although it is said to be the Savagnin Rose of the Jura and also said to be the Traminer, formerly planted quite widely and now replaced by the more aromatic clone Gewurztraminer, it is not absolutely identical to either one. An experimental vineyard in southern Alsace has planted different clones of Gewurztraminer, Traminer, Klevener and Savagnin Rose, all on the same rootstocks and the same soil and it can be seen that there are subtle differences between them all, although the family resemblances are strong.

The Klevener has been the speciality of the village of Heiligenstein for the last 200 years, although it was discouraged under German rule and not authorised for replanting, so the area dwindled. When the list of varietals for the appellation was drawn up in Brussels in 1971, Klevener was overlooked and only strong local protest secured the appellation. Around 100 hectares have been delimited as potential vineyard area for Klevener, on clay slopes around the village. At present the village grows about one-third Sylvaner, but this is slowly changing in favour of the Klevener.

The grapes are deep pink/bronze skinned and the wine produced has a little of the spice of a Gewurztraminer, without being strongly scented. Klevener generally produces better than Gewurztraminer in poor years, although the Gewurztraminer does better in very good years. The yield for Klevener is generally quite low, at around 40 hectolitres per hectare.

Klevener is soft, dry, with medium weight and length, less alcoholic than Gewurztraminer, with a soft, earthy, mildly aromatic flavour. It is excellent as an aperitif and could also stand up to fish or light meat dishes. It is a very attractive wine, generally at its best between one and five years from the vintage, although in good years it can keep for 10 to 20 years.

KLEVENER DE HEILIGENSTEIN

CAVE CO-OPÉRATIVE D'ANDLAU, Barr
Co-operative
1985 ①
Light, flowery, spicy nose. Light, spicy fruit on the palate, leaner style, lightweight, elegant, floral, but without great depth. Clean, well-made.

JEAN HEYWANG, Heiligenstein
Propriétaire viticulteur

Two cuvées since 1985, one of young vines, one of older vines designated Cuvée Particulière.
1985/6 ① ★
Perfumed nose, soft, gently spicy, lightweight, with good balancing acidity. Medium length, drinks well when young.
Cuvée Particulière (1985/6) ② ★★/★★★
More pronounced perfumed, almost smoky nose. Firmer, spicy fruit on palate, drier, fuller flavour, more weighty. Attractive when young but ages well. I have tasted this wine back to the 1976 vintage, which is superb. Even in lesser years such as 1984, Jean Heywang makes an exciting wine. Recommended.

RENÉ MECKERT, Heiligenstein
Propriétaire viticulteur
1986 ① / ② ★
Quite honeyed, spicy nose, almost rosewater/turkish delight. A

creamier, rounder, fatter style, gently spicy, smoky, with
balancing acidity. Well-made wine, drinking well when young,
but would age well.

A. RUFF, Heiligenstein
Propriétaire viticulteur
Cuvée Particulière (1986) ☐1

Light, spicy nose, not very positive. Harder flavour, hints of
flowery fruit, but less character, rather dull, heavy, less fruity. A
little lacking in charm.

Schwendehiesel, Cuvée du Millesime (1986) ☐2

Much more positive, spicy fruit on nose and palate, more
concentrated, with a slightly honeyed, peach-flavour. Soft,
attractive, lightly-spiced fruit, still quite youthful and would
improve with another year in bottle.

KAEFFERKOPF

The vineyard of Kaefferkopf, to the south of Ammerschwihr, covers an area of 63 hectares. The first mention of the vineyards is in archives dated 1328, when it was known as Zem Kefersberg. An agricultural survey in 1866 specified that Kaefferkopf produced top quality wines, much prized on the market place and in 1931 a local syndicate decided that wines from Gewurztraminer, Riesling, Tokay-Pinot Gris, Muscat and Pinot Blanc, or a blend of any of these varieties, could be sold simply with the name Kaefferkopf, without any mention of variety. This denomination was officially delimited in 1932 and confirmed as an Appellation in 1966, one of a few 'vineyard' Appellations which do not mention the grape variety. Several vignerons still produce 'Kaefferkopf'; J. B. Adam from 80 per cent Gewurztraminer and 20 per cent Tokay, Maurice Schoech from 100 per cent Gewurztraminer and Sick-Dreyer from Pinot Blanc.

The soil is of limestone and clay and is quite varied, as too are the aspects, some parts of the vineyard being more favoured than others. The altitude of the vines is between 240 and 320 metres and the best wines are from the Gewurztraminer, although some very attractive Tokay-Pinot Gris and Riesling wines can also be found.

KAEFFERKOPF

JEAN-BAPTISTE ADAM, Ammerschwihr
Négociant
Kaefferkopf (1985)　②　★
> Soft, floral nose, oily, apricot, spicy. Solid, spicy, peachy fruit on the palate, with spicy, smoky, ripe fruit. Quite weighty, earthy, rich, with good length of flavour, which develops well in glass. Very attractive. For medium term drinking. 4-7 years.

MAURICE SCHOECH, Ammerschwihr
Propriétaire viticulteur
Kaefferkopf (1985/86)

   Maurice Schoech's Kaefferkopf is made purely from
   Gewurztraminer, and is therefore under the Gewurztraminer
   section of the book.

PIERRE SPARR & SES FILS, Sigolsheim
Négociant
Kaefferkopf Réserve (1986)   ② / ③ ★

   Attractive, aromatic, spicy, floral nose. Spicy, gently-rounded
   fruit on the palate, aromatic, discreet, gentle, with good length of
   elegant flavour. Dry but rich and aromatic. Made from a blend
   of Riesling and Gewurztraminer. For early to medium term
   drinking. 2-6 years.

EDELZWICKER

Edelzwicker is the designation given to a wine produced from a blend of different varieties. A century ago it was rare to find a plot of land entirely planted with a single variety and the wines were blended as a matter of course. In fact, in the last century many of these wines were denoted the second best wine produced in Alsace (after Tokay) and were produced under the name of the grower or vineyard. This still exists in the case of some Kaefferkopf wines, which are often blended and often considered by the grower to be one of his best wines.

Blended wines of this type were known as Gentil in the last century – a rather confusing name, which seems to have been in wide use to denote a 'noble' wine, and which is still in use in some Alsace villages today. Unfortunately in the nineteenth century some merchants in Riquewihr added eau-de-vie to their Gentils, then stretched the wine with some more common grapes, which harmed the reputation of this name.

The original Appellation Contrôlée laws differentiated between Zwicker and Edelzwicker, the former being used for blends that were not entirely from noble varieties. Zwicker was later discontinued, and more varieties such as Sylvaner 'ennobled'. This century has seen the disappearance of many of the grape varieties which were traditionally grown in mixed vineyards, which included Aligoté, Elbling, Trollinger, Olber, Muller-Thürgau, Gamay à jus blanc, Pinot Meunier, Bouquettraube, Chardonnay (Auvernat), Goldriesling and Knipperlé. Of these, Knipperlé, also known as Kleiner Rauchsling, Ortlieber or Petit Mielleux, was widely planted, producing a full bodied wine, more mellow in character than Chasselas, which has largely replaced it. It was resistant to oidium and a good producer in all weather conditions, but the wine did not keep well. There are still patches of old vines in Alsace planted with these 'ignoble' varieties, the wine from which is sold as Edelzwicker. These vineyards are, however, being gradually phased out.

Edelzwicker is blended mainly from Auxerrois, Pinot Blanc, Sylvaner and Chasselas and is often a rather light, pleasant, but somewhat bland, quaffing wine. However, a good number of vignerons produce a more interesting wine, using the blend as a means of disposing of second pressings from their better varieties and the wine from awkward varieties such as Muscat in years where it has failed to ripen sufficiently to produce a wine in its own right. Edelzwicker is sometimes put into the new oak casks, to remove any traces of new oak flavour from the wood before it can be used for the better cuvées, because with few exceptions the winemaker does not wish to have the pure grape flavour of his varietals sullied with the flavour of the oak cask.

Edelzwicker is largely used in the region as a carafe wine, and is often sold in litre bottles. Some winemakers prefer to use a brand name, in which case the word Edelzwicker does not always appear on the label.

Around 500 hectares of vineyards are planted with grapes used to make Edelzwicker, which accounts for about 5 per cent of the wine produced in Alsace. The percentage is decreasing in favour of Pinot Blanc.

Edelzwicker is best when young, between one and three years from the vintage. It is an excellent aperitif wine, and some of the more interesting spicy examples would be excellent with charcuterie or light fish dishes.

EDELZWICKER

JEAN HEYWANG, Heiligenstein
Propriétaire viticulteur
Edelzwicker (1985)   ☐1
> Soft, spicy nose, not very positive. Quite high acidity on the palate, with some spicy fruit underlying. Pleasant, fresh, but a little anonymous.

OBRECHT, Wettolsheim
Co-operative
Edelzwicker (1984)   ☐1
> Soft, honeyed nose and palate. Clean, lightweight, soft, with a little balancing acidity. Fresh, rather short, anonymous.

PFLUGER-HAEGEL, Dambach-la-Ville
Propriétaire viticulteur
Edelzwicker (n/v)　[1]
Spicy, floral nose, quite full and buttery. Soft, honeyed fruit on
the palate, quite gentle, attractive, mellow. Gentle, soft, dry
white, not very Alsace in character, but quite attractive.

CAVE DU ROESSELSTEIN, Turckheim
Négociant
Cuvée Roesselstein (n/v)　[1]
Soft, flowery, spicy nose, aromatic, floral. Light, soft, gentle fruit
on the palate, aromatic, fresh, without much acidity. Slightly
sulphury. Gentle, pleasant, a little short.

ROLLY GASSMANN, Rorschwihr
Propriétaire viticulteur
Edelzwicker (1986)　[2] ★★
Attractive, flowery nose. Clean, light fruit on the palate, with
crisp, balancing acidity and an attractive, light spiciness. Very
clean, fresh, with a slight earthy spiciness and good length.
Well-made wine with some character.

DOMAINE SCHLUMBERGER, Guebwiller

Propriétaire viticulteur

Cristal Doré (n/v)   1

Light, fresh, gently dry wine, with good balancing acidity. Clean, fresh, lightweight, pleasant but quite short.

Schlumberger Réserve (n/v)   2 ★★

A special 'reserve' cuvée, with some Gewurztraminer, a touch of Riesling, on a base of Sylvaner and Pinot Blanc. Full gold colour. Very spicy, floral, honeyed nose, with Gewurztraminer spice. Soft, rich, spicy fruit on the palate, hints of grapefruit, gently spicy, peachy, with a certain leanness. Nice mature fruit, with very individual character and quite elegant and distinguished.

MAURICE SCHOECH, Ammerschwihr

Propriétaire viticulteur

Edelzwicker (1985)   1 ★★

From a mixed patch of old vines, which include Knipperlé, Sylvaner, Pinot Blanc and Chasselas. Quite spicy, soft nose and palate, with gentle, ripe, peachy, spicy fruit and a little acidity to balance. Dry, mild and mellow, with good length and weight. Plenty of character.

PIERRE SPARR & SES FILS, Sigolsheim

Négociant

Rayon d'Alsace (n/v)   1 / 2 ★

Soft, peachy fruit nose. Attractive, clean, soft fruit on the palate, with the slight toffee fudge flavour of Auxerrois, mild, well balanced, with light acidity and gentle, warm, floral, dry fruit. Well-made wine with plenty of character.

ALFRED WANTZ, Mittelbergheim
Propriétaire viticulteur
Gentil (1985) ☐1
Not very positive nose or palate, slightly cardboardy, flat, with light, gentle fruit, but without very positive character. Rather dull, disappointing.

MAISON WIEDERHIRN, Riquewihr
Propriétaire viticulteur
Réserve Fruits de Mer (1986) ☐2
Floral, minerally nose. Lighter, drier style, with quite lemony, tart acidity and lightweight, fresh, floral, herbal fruit. Intended to accompany seafood, light, fresh style, maybe a little heavy on the acidity.

ALSACE WILLM, Barr
Négociant
Edelzwicker (1983) ☐1
Soft, spicy nose, slightly honeyed, appley. Soft, ripe, spicy fruit on the palate, honeyed, pleasant, but a little tired. Probably very attractive a year or two before. Recommended, if you find a younger vintage.

CRÉMANT D'ALSACE

Sparkling wines have been made in the Alsace region for many years, but it is only since 24 August 1976 that an official designation and appellation were finally settled. Most of the production is white, from Riesling, Pinot Blanc, Pinot Noir, Pinot Gris, Auxerrois or Chardonnay, in whatever combinations the grower desires. There is also a small amount of rosé Crémant, exclusively from the Pinot Noir.

A date is fixed annually for the commencement of the harvest, usually several days earlier for wines intended for Crémant than for other wines, since a higher acidity level is required. The grower must declare his crop at the time of the vintage as 'vin destiné à l'élaboration de Crémant d'Alsace' and file papers to show the quantity harvested. The minimum natural sugar at harvest must be 145 grams per litre, giving a potential alcohol of 8·5° and a record must be made at the press-house, showing for each pressing the varieties, weight of must, potential alcohol, origin of grapes and volume of juice obtained. No more than 100 litres may be extracted per 150 kilos of grapes.

The still wine may not be bottled for secondary fermentation in the bottle before 1 January of the year following the vintage and the wine must spend a minimum of nine months on the lees before degorgement. The finished pressure in the bottle must be at least four atmospheres of pressure at 20°C.

Production is on the increase, but sadly the quality is often uneven, for a variety of reasons. Firstly, the wine is very popular with local tourists and is often produced with price in mind rather than quality. Some producers are sticking literally to the minimum requirements of the law, selling the wine when it is still young and green, in time for the following Christmas! The quality of the grapes used for the manufacture of Crémant is often low: growers can get a far better price for their higher quality varieties and so are reluctant to sell them for Crémant production, the bulk of grapes used being Pinot Blanc and Auxerrois.

But whilst a great many rather bland wines are produced, there are some excellent quality Crémants available from

Alsace. Most of the co-operatives produce Crémant, and many small growers make limited quantities to add to their repertoire of wines offered. Most Crémant is not vintage dated and is sold when it is ready to drink. Although it can often benefit from six months or a year's ageing, it is not intended for very long keeping. The volume is increasing annually and now stands at some 83,637 hectolitres per year, from 985 hectares of vines, representing 7·8 per cent of the total volume (1987 vintage figures from CIVA). There are almost 1,500 labels of Crémant d'Alsace marketed, many in very small volumes and some 80 per cent of the volume of sales comes from a mere 150 labels.

Crémant d'Alsace is nearly always dry and is the ideal aperitif, generally softer and earthier than other French sparkling wines, with a gentle fruit and subtle, floral flavour.

CRÉMANT D'ALSACE

CAVE CO-OPÉRATIVE DE BENNWIHR & ENVIRONS,
Bennwihr
Co-operative
Brut (NV)   ② ★

Good mousse. Attractive, fresh, slightly creamy nose. Lovely classic, soft, clean, fresh fruit, crisp, dry style, young and fresh, with good length of flavour. Well-made.

PAUL BLANCK, Kientzheim
Propriétaire viticulteur
Brut (1985)   ② / ③

Their Crémant is always made as a single vintage. Light, fresh
fruit, good mousse, dry, quite lean wine, almost herbal, sappy.
Medium length. Quite herbaceous wine.

BOTT FRÈRES, Ribeauvillé
Propriétaire viticulteur
Cuvée Nicole (n/v)   ③ ★

Good fine mousse. Floral nose, not very positive. Lovely, soft,
creamy, gentle fruit, with a slightly smoky spiciness. Mild,
easy-drinking, dry, but not unduly so. Very attractive, soft,
well-made wine.

DOPFF AU MOULIN, Riquewihr
Négociant
Cuvée Extra (now called Cuvée Julien)   ① / ② ★

The basic sparkling wine from this firm, which has long
specialised in Crémant production. Made from 100% Pinot Blanc,
with a small dosage of ½% to 1%, depending on the vintage,
although the vintage is not specified on the label. Good mousse.
Soft, lightly spicy, creamy nose and palate, soft, fruity, dry, but
quite gentle style, with good length and flavour. Well-made.

Wild Brut (1983)   ① / ② ★

The same base wine as the Cuvée Julien, but with no dosage and
sold as a single vintage. Crisper, drier, lighter style, clean, more
herbal. Very fresh, giving the impression of a lighter wine. Good
aperitif style.

Blanc de Noirs (1983)   ② / ③ ★★★

Made purely from Pinot Noir, with a light dosage of about ½%, this wine has a lovely full, earthy fruit, dry, but fuller, with very good Pinot character, somewhat reminiscent of Blanc de Noirs Champagne. Very attractive soft pinot flavour. A wine which improves with a few years bottle age. Dopff also make a rosé from Pinot Noir, with a little more dosage than the white.

Cuvée Bartholdi (1983) ③ ★★

A special cuvée, named after the creator of the Statue of Liberty
and produced for the New York festival. Still dry, but with a
richer weight of fruit, good balancing acidity and more body.
Lovely rich, powerful, fruit, well-balanced, more solid style, with
good length of flavour. Improves with a few years bottle age.
Made from Pinot Blanc.

LUCIEN FREYERMUTH, Dambach-la-Ville

Négociant

Brut (n/v) ②

Good mousse. The sulphur is overwhelming on the nose, but the
palate is gentle and attractive, with soft, warm fruit and less
noticeable acidity. Gentle, dry, mild style, with good length of
flavour.

JÉROME GESCHICKT, Ammerschwihr

Propriétaire viticulteur

Brut (n/v) ②

Made from a blend of Riesling, Pinot Gris and Pinot Blanc.
Light mousse. Quite gentle, spicy, soft fruit on the nose and
palate, clean, quite mild style, with light acidity and less positive
mousse. Gentle, pleasant.

LOUIS GISSELBRECHT, Dambach-la-Ville
Négociant
Brut (n/v) ②

Very light mousse, which disappears quickly. Light, appley fruit on nose and palate, fresh, clean, very lightweight. Dry but without much acidity. Clean, well-made, but a little bland.

WILLY GISSELBRECHT, Dambach-la-Ville
Négociant
Pinot Noir (rosé) (n/v) ② ★

Light rose colour. Good fine mousse. Attractive soft fruit on the palate, with the sweetness of Pinot Noir and almost raspberry fruit. Dry, but with soft, red fruit flavour and good length. Gentle, attractive.

BARON DE HOEN, Beblenheim
Co-operative
Blanc de Blancs Brut (n/v) ② ★★

Good mousse. Attractive, soft, ripe, creamy nose. More weighty fruit, soft, ripe, with a little balancing acidity. Gentle, well-made, with good length and plenty of character. Attractive classic style.

MARC KREYDENWEISS, Andlau
Propriétaire viticulteur
Brut (n/v) ② ★

Made from a blend of Auxerrois, Riesling and Pinot Gris. Good mousse, light, lemony, floral, spicy nose and palate, honeyed, clean, with good weight of soft dry fruit and clean balancing acidity. Dry but quite spicy style, with good length of flavour. Well-made.

MICHEL LAUGEL, Marlenheim
Négociant
Strohl is an alias of Michel Laugel.
Brut (n/v) ☒
> Light mousse, but persistent. Gentle clean light fruit on the palate, mild, floral, with good balancing acidity and medium length. Soft, fresh, well-made wine.

PAUL MITTNACHT, VIEILLE CAVE DE CICOGNE,
Westhalten
Propriétaire viticulteur
Blanc de Blancs Réserve Brut (1983) ☒
> Light mousse. Attractive, light, appley, fruit nose, with warm, soft fruit on the palate, a little short, lacking acidity. Soft, mild, less fruity style, warm and rather flat. Probably better 2–3 years ago.

MURÉ, CLOS ST. LANDELIN, Rouffach
Négociant
Brut '0' ☒
> Made from 100% Riesling, with no dosage. Good mousse, dry, clean, very fresh, almost herbal fruit. Drier and with more prominent acidity than many and light herbal, floral finish.
Brut (n/v) ☒
> As above, but with about 5 grams per litre dosage, which does not appear to make the wine taste sweeter, but brings out the riesling character more positively. Dry, floral Riesling, with good mousse, dry, very fresh, with quite prominent acidity.

PIERRE SPARR & SES FILS, Sigolsheim
Négociant
Brut Reserve, Blanc de Blancs (n/v) ☒ ★
> Good mousse. Fresh, light, grapey nose, not very positive. Spicy fruit on the palate, lightweight, clean, pleasant. Dry and fresh, without too noticeable acidity. Good aperitif style.

JEAN-BAPTISTE THOMANN, Ammerschwihr
Propriétaire viticulteur
Blanc de Blancs (n/v) ☒ ★
> Soft, honeyed, creamy nose and palate, spicy, very soft, with light balancing acidity. Dry, quite warm and earthy, with a nice spicy finish. Soft, gentle, creamy style, attractive.

ALFRED WANTZ, Mittelbergheim
Propriétaire viticulteur
Brut (n/v)   2 ★

Good mousse. Light, fresh nose, with soft, minerally, gentle fruit on the palate. Leaner, herbal, dry style, quite lightweight, with good balance and length. Nicely made wine with some character.

WOLFBERGER, Eguisheim
Co-operative
Brut (1983)   2 ★

Very attractive presentation, with a decorated bottle. Good mousse, full-flavoured, creamy style, with good weight of fruit, light acidity and fresh, clean, ripe fruit flavour. Lightly spicy, earthy, solid style, but very fresh and clean. Well-made.

VINS DE LIQUEUR and VINS DE PAILLE

Alsace was once famous as a producer of some of the best sweet wines of France. These took the form both of Vins de Liqueur, made from very ripe grapes of the Chasselas, Muscat and 'Gentil' varieties and of *Strohweine, Vins des Rois* or *vins de paille*, where ripe grapes were laid to dry on straw until around March the following year and then crushed to make wine. This practice was said to have been invented by Dagar, the mayor of Colmar in 1764. Only the best healthy, ripe grapes from the best varieties could be used and grapes were checked weekly to remove any mouldy or rotten berries. As an alternative to laying the grapes on straw, they were also suspended on threads in attics of houses, with the doors and windows left open for aeration except during frosty weather. The finished juice would represent about one-tenth of the potential juice at harvest and the wine, which needed very long ageing, was reputed to be very fine, somewhat similar to a Tokay Essencia. The best crus of these wines included Colmar, Kayserberg, Kientzheim, Ammerschwihr, Ribeauvillé, Turckheim, Ottrott and Ollwiller. Wolxheim and Heiligenstein were also especially cited for their Muscats.

Sadly, the fashion for this style of wine, which was produced in many wine-producing regions of France, died out at the beginning of this century. However, a few growers are experimenting with wines of this style, mainly for their personal consumption, and André Ostertag of Epfig has made a very interesting *vin de paille* in 1987. Let us hope these wines are due for a come-back.

EAUX-DE-VIE AND FRUIT LIQUEURS

It was common practice in the Middle Ages for farmhouses and homesteads to have their own domestic still. Usually these were found in homes nearest to a stream or source of fresh water, which could be used for cooling. Most distillations were of the marc, or skins and pips left after pressing, or of the lees, the yeasty sediment left at the bottom of vats during fermentation. These were known as *Drusenbrantwein* and had a very strong aroma. They were excellent digestives and were considered to cure many ailments.

In the sixteenth century Alsace fruit spirits gained recognition throughout France and Europe and, in 1583, Strasbourg exported 2,057 hectolitres of eaux-de-vie, the most important purchasers being the Germans, the Dutch and the English. In the seventeenth century, with political unrest, the industry largely died out and many homesteads and stills were destroyed. The nineteenth century saw a revival, with wine lees and Gewurztraminer making the most popular eaux-de-vie.

Now there are at least 36 different fruits, buds and other often quite peculiar distillations, including such diverse flavours as celery, pine, ginger and rowan berries. A licence to distil can be quite easily obtained and many producers, both large and small, boast one or several eaux-de-vie to add to their already large range of products.

The best eaux-de-vie are produced from local fruit, such as William pears, cherries and the small golden Mirabelle plums from Lorraine. Many are also produced from fruits imported from other parts of France, or even from abroad. Unfortunately good fruit is expensive and many producers buy over-ripe or imperfect fruits, which are less costly. It is also said that fruits can be 'stretched' by the addition of apples – illegal, but then apples are so much less expensive. To test the quality of the fruit flavour and to detect adulterations, a little eau-de-vie is rubbed between the palms of the hands and then sniffed. This will show the perfume of the fruit and the intensity of fruit flavour.

To make eau-de-vie, the chosen fruit is crushed and fermented in the same way as wine. With vegetal substances, the starch breaks down into sugar, which can then be fermented. Because the sugar content is a very low percentage in many of the fruits, the finished fruit wine may only achieve 4 or 5 per cent alcohol. This fruit wine is then distilled in a pot still and occasionally aged before bottling. The colour must be clear, so ageing takes place in glass vats rather than in wood, although one can occasionally find Marc de Gewurztraminer that has been aged in wood. Marc de Gewurztraminer is covered by the Appellation Contrôlée laws and comes from a fermentation of the skins and pips of Gewurztraminer grapes grown within the delimited region of Alsace and distilled within the region. The distillation takes place in a pot still, whose maximum volume is laid down as not being capable of processing more than 50 hectolitres of primary matter per 24 hours. The finished marc must obtain a maximum 68° Gay Lussac (percentage alcohol by volume) and must be of a minimum of 45° when bottled and sold. About 350 hectolitres of pure alcohol equivalent are produced each year (about 750 to 800 hectolitres at selling strength).

Most eaux-de-vie are products of a single vintage and, contrary to popular belief, they can improve with ageing. It was possible to find vintage dated spirits until comparatively recently, but this practice now seems to have ceased.

A spirit which has appeared in much larger quantities in recent times is Fine d'Alsace, a brandy made from the wine, rather than the skins, pips or lees. This is because of the rise in popularity of Crémant d'Alsace, where only the first 100 litres of juice per 150 kilos of grapes may be used to make sparkling wine. This leaves a quantity of juice that has no appellation, not even that of Edelzwicker and this is fermented, distilled, and usually aged in wood, to give a very pleasant brandy.

As well as Marc de Gewurztraminer, which has a very distinctive bouquet and flavour, it is also possible to find marc from Pinot Noir and Riesling, although these would be far harder to identify as far as tracing the varietal character!

Many of the flavours used for eaux-de-vie are also used to produce liqueurs, sweetened flavoured spirits, often the colour of the fruit used and sold at a lower strength, usually around 30°. Some of these make very attractive additions to Crémant, rather in the manner of a *kir royale*, but most are a little too sweet and sticky to drink on their own.

SOME GROWERS

LÉON BEYER, EGUISHEIM

The Beyer family have had vineyards in the Eguisheim region since 1580. The current firm was founded in 1867. As well as the grapes from their own vineyards, which cover 20 hectares, including parts of the Grand Cru Schoenenberg, they buy in grapes from other growers, controlling quality and maturity of the grapes on arrival at the press-house and separating the better grapes for their reserve cuvée. Their wines are always vinified dry, with less than two grams of residual sugar per litre, except for the occasional Vendange Tardive or Sélection de Grains Nobles wine produced in an outstanding vintage. Wine storage is in their picturesque underground cellars, which date from 1865 and which are six metres below ground level, at a constant temperature of 10°. Their wines may be found on all the top restaurant lists throughout France. Léon Beyer and his son, Marc, frequently travel both at home and abroad to spread the message of their wines. The house style is for firm, full-flavoured dry wines, with elegance and good lasting abilities. The better cuvées, such as Cuvée Particulière, Les Écaillers, and Comtes d'Eguisheim, are made from their own vineyards. Vendange Tardive and Sélection de Grains Nobles wines are made in the best vintages and these also are of a firm, quite austere style when young, requiring long ageing. All their wines blossom well with age and show remarkable power and consistency.

BOTT FRÈRES, RIBEAUVILLÉ

The Bott family have 15 hectares of vineyard around the town of Ribeauvillé. The wines are traditionally made and the aim is to produce wines which are ready to drink when still quite young, only two to three years' stocks being maintained. The wines are matured in large old wooden cuves of between 100 and 160 hectolitres for six months after fermentation and racking, and are usually bottled with a few grams of residual sugar. The aim here is to produce wines as naturally as possible, with as little treatment as possible. The best wines, designated Réserve Exceptionelle, are made from the free run juice of their premium varieties.

ALBERT BOXLER, NIEDERMORSCHWIHR

The Domaine Albert Boxler is run by Albert and his son Jean Marc, who have a total of 10 hectares, specialising in Riesling, with some Gewurztraminer and Tokay on the richer, deeper soils of the region. Their vineyard holdings include some Grand Cru Sommerberg and Brand and the wines are made as naturally as possible, using the natural yeasts of the region. Albert Boxler spent some time in America during his youth, but returned to Alsace during the depression to take up the family vineyards. As well as their elegant, aromatic Sommerberg and firmer, longer-lived Brand Rieslings, they also produce very good Vendange Tardive wines in the better vintages.

GAEC MARCEL DEISS, BERGHEIM

The Deiss family own 20 hectares, split up into around 120 different patches of vines along a 20 kilometre stretch of land between Saint Hippolyte and Sigolsheim. They are strong exponents of the importance of *terroir* and vinify wines from each soil type separately, giving an enormous range of wines, including at least eight different Rieslings each vintage. As well as the six employees working for the family, there are the family members themselves, who take a fierce pride in their wines, and each strives to further the firm's image and reputation for quality. Jean Michel Deiss looks after the cellar and his father takes care of the vineyards, each ensuring that the best use is made of their vineyard sites, which include holdings in the two Grand Cru vineyards Altenberg de Bergheim and Schoenenbourg of Riquewihr. The wines are traditionally vinified, although Jean Michel Deiss has installed temperature control in order to regulate the temperature at fermentation, which he adjusts according to the nature of the grape variety, the vintage and the soil of each wine's provenance.

The Deiss family produce some very good, late harvest wines and their top wines generally take a long time to mature, but can be very long lived.

DOPFF AU MOULIN, RIQUEWIHR

Jean-Daniel Dopff, a minister's son, settled in Riquewihr as an innkeeper and baker in the seventeenth century. His son became a master cooper and his descendents became Gourmets, or wine brokers, and then wine producers. In 1900, Julien Dopff attended a demonstration of the Méthode Champenoise at the Universal Exhibition in Paris and was struck by the idea of sparkling wine. He trained for two years in Epernay and even opened an office in the Champagne region, where he sold his wines. With the Appellation Contrôlée laws, he concentrated on the Alsace region, and tried cuvées of different grapes. Until the AC for Crémant, he was one of the few producers of sparkling wines in the region. Julien Dopff was also one of the first advocates of the flute bottle in 1913. To prove the ability of the wine to age well in this shape of bottle, he wagered that his wine could journey safely from Alsace to Australia and back again without harm. He won his bet. The house of Dopff own 70 hectares around Riquewihr, Turckheim and Colmar, including 13 hectares of Grand Cru vineyards. These vineyards supply 25 per cent of their needs, the remainder being bought in from around 500 growers, always purchased as grapes rather than as wine. After pressing, the juice is centrifuged, then fermented either in stainless steel or in lined cement vats. After fermentation the wines are aged in wood, the simpler wines being bottled the spring after the vintage, the better wines being bottled in the autumn, then kept for a further year or more in bottle before release. Dopff produce 600,000 bottles of sparkling wine a year, and control an important percentage of the Crémant market. They also distil fruit liqueurs, as well as Marc de Gewurztraminer, and Fine d'Alsace, produced from the juice left over after the best has been used for Crémant. The wines are carefully made, whether the 'simple' range, with the distinctive diamond shaped labels, or the finer wines from their own vineyards, which can be truly superb.

DOMAINE THÉO FALLER, WEINBACH, KAYSERBERG

The house and the walled vineyard in front of the house belonged to a convent until 1789 and then were purchased by a lawyer from Colmar in 1791. His great-granddaughter sold the *domaine* to the Faller family in 1898. The estate comprises 23 hectares, including the four hectare Clos des Capucins by the house, around 10 hectares of Grand Cru Schlossberg and the remainder near Kientzheim, Kayserberg and Ammerschwihr. 40 per cent of the vineyards are planted with Riesling, 30 per cent with Gewurtztraminer, 10 per cent with Tokay. The custom of the house is to vinify each cask separately, even where there is more than one cask from the same vineyard. The wines are not generally sold with any indication of the cask number, but purchasers have the opportunity to choose their cask at the property. It is, justifiably, a very popular *domaine* and during a recent visit there were parties of diverse nationalities converging from all directions to taste their wines. We were looked after by Madame Faller's charming daughter, whilst Madame was occupied with a party of *sommeliers* from Champagne. Bottles and personnel whisked in and out of each room of the house, as each group tasted the tremendous range of wines produced, passing each bottle along to the next tasting. Madame Faller has taken control of the estate since the death of her husband, Théo, and runs the *domaine* with tremendous enthusiasm and love of her wines. Here also they have purchased a pneumatic Bucher press in 1987. Vinification is traditional, with each cask carefully monitored and the Faller family show a love for and familiarity with each cask of their wine.

JEAN HEYWANG, HEILIGENSTEIN

The Heywang family have five hectares of vineyard around the picturesque village of Heiligenstein, including a small amount of land on the Grand Cru Kirchberg at Barr, planted with old Gewurztraminer vines dating from 1952 and 1956. The vines are pruned to one arcure to give small yields. Vinification is traditional, in the old wooden vats in their underground cellar, which is permanently at a temperature of between 8° and

12°C. In 1987, however, they purchased a Willmes press, a high expense for a small grower, but one which they feel will be fully justified by the quality of juice extracted. Sulphur is only present through the use of *méchage*, the burning of sulphur sticks inside the empty vats to disinfect before filling, and the level of SO_2 in the finished wines is therefore low. Most of their vineyards lie on rich, deep, heavy, clay, limestone and mica soil, which is suited to the more aromatic varieties and to their local village speciality, Klevener de Heiligenstein. They have just under a hectare of this unique varietal, of which they now produce two cuvées. At Heywang, there is the happy marriage between the best traditional practices of the region and the best advances of modern science.

ANDRÉ KIENTZLER, RIBEAUVILLÉ

André Kientzler has 10 hectares around the town of Ribeauvillé. Viticulture and vinification show great attention to the all-important details. André Kientzler carefully monitors the production of all his vineyards, firstly by pruning the vines short, then by observing the size of the potential crop after flowering and by removing any excess clusters during the summer months to ensure maximum concentration in the remaining grape bunches. In the cellar too, this care is continued, with a pneumatic press and temperature controlled fermentation in traditional wooden vats. He has experimented with oak-ageing his Auxerrois. He is one of few growers to bottle a straight Chasselas, more usually blended with other varieties to form Edelzwicker. Part of his vineyards are on the Grand Cru sites Geisberg and Kirchberg, where the yield is small and the wines extremely concentrated. He has produced some very good late-picked wines, as Vendange Tardive, Sélection de Grains Nobles, and also in the form of a very unusual *Vin de Glace*, or *Eiswein*, picked on 24 December 1986, with a very intense, honeyed riesling fruit. André Kientzler is a very modest and retiring man, passionately interested in the quality of his wines and producing some of the best wines of the region.

MARC KREYDENWEISS, ANDLAU

Marc Kreydenweiss's grandfather, Fernand Gresser, was one of the pioneers of bottling at source, and the *domaine*, in the less fashionable Bas Rhin, has always specialised in Riesling, producing wines capable of long ageing. The *domaine* covers just under ten hectares, including three Grand Cru sites, Kastelberg, Wiebelsberg, and Moenchberg, all facing the picturesque village of Andlau. The Kastelberg vineyard, immediately behind the cellars, produces the *domaine*'s best wine, from a unique schist soil, steeply sloping. In spite of a precipitous slope, at an angle of 45°, Marc Kreydenweiss plants his vines north to south, running from top to bottom of the slope. This enables the sun to reach both sides of the rows of vines, and therefore produces grapes with a higher oechsle, by about ten degrees, than would be produced by planting east to west. Thus his vineyard is not terraced, and all the vineyard work, pruning, training, and picking, has to be carried out laboriously by hand. Vines are planted in high density, up to ten thousand vines per hectare, to give lower production per vine and therefore a more concentrated flavour. Pruning is very short and the crop size is further reduced by summer pruning. Herbage replaces humus, which is scarce on this soil and the vines get used to surface vegetation after three to four years, the roots seeking deeper and extracting more mineral content from the soil. The ground cover also helps to prevent soil erosion. Some chalk is added every few years, to raise the pH, and prevent chlorosis.

The care in the cellar is just as immaculate. Although the cellar is old, with the traditional large oak casks, Marc has introduced temperature control by passing pipes through the vats, carrying water from the Andlau river, which runs just behind the cellar. The natural yeasts are used for fermentation, and each vineyard area is vinified separately, keeping the cuvées of wine from younger vines separately for his generic wines, and only using the best vats for his top cuvées. Sulphur levels are kept to a minimum. He is also experimenting with the use of new oak to give more interest to Sylvaner, and has produced a couple of vintages of late-picked Auxerrois. (This is not a variety entitled to be labelled Vendange Tardive, but does produce very attractive, rich, peachy, bitter-orange flavours when late-picked.) There is also a small amount of

Crémant d'Alsace produced, around five to six thousand bottles a year, from a blend of 50 per cent Auxerrois, 40 per cent Riesling and 10 per cent Tokay. He has just replaced his horizontal Vaslin press with a Bucher, or bladder press, which gives a clearer, cleaner juice, and will, he hopes, give even better results.

A Vendange Tardive Gewurztraminer was produced for the first time in 1983, a very rich wine, which was unusually vinified dry, and still needs many years' ageing. Gewurztraminer, Riesling and Tokay were picked later in 1985 to produce Vendange Tardive wines and, in 1987, for the first time, a Sélection de Grains Nobles was produced from Gewurztraminer, picked at 140° oechsle and fermented at a low temperature.

Since 1984, the *domaine* has introduced artist's labels, commissioning a different local artist each year to depict the style of the vintage.

Care at all stages of the operation, from the vineyard to the marketing of the finished product, is the order of the day, coupled with a love of fine wines, an enquiring mind and an immense enthusiasm both for the wines of the *domaine* and of the Alsace region.

FRÉDÉRIC MALLO, HUNAWIHR

Frédéric Mallo has seven hectares around the village of Hunawihr, including half a hectare of Grand Cru Mandelberg, planted with Gewurztraminer, and one-and-a-half hectares of Rosacker, planted with Riesling. The Rosacker vineyard is adjacent to Trimbach's famous Clos Sainte Hune. Frédéric Mallo is aiming to produce a 'tender' style of wine in all varieties and his wines are elegant and clean, racy but never heavy. He is a great enthusiast, who talks nineteen to the dozen about his beloved wines. His Rieslings and Tokays in particular are highly recommended.

DOMAINE OSTERTAG, EPFIG

The Ostertag family have been vignerons at Epfig for generations. The wines are now made by André Ostertag, an immensely enthusiastic young winemaker who is constantly seeking for new ideas. The Ostertags also have bought a pneumatic press and have installed temperature control into the traditional wooden vats, as well as adding some new stainless steel vats to their cellar. The wines from the Domaine are designated either *fruit* or *terroir*, according to their provenance. The *fruit* wines are lighter, earlier-drinking wines, designed to show the character of the grape varietal, which are bottled before the summer following the vintage. The *terroir* wines, designed to show the particularities of their vineyard site in addition to the grape character, are more complex wines, bottled the autumn after the vintage and intended for long ageing. The *terroir* wines come from the vineyards of Fronholz, a quartz soil, producing somewhat austere wines, less charming in their youth; Heissenberg, a warm granite slope, giving a more herbal wine; and Muenchberg, a Grand Cru site of red sandstone, producing very elegant wine. André Ostertag has experimented with the use of oak for both fermentation and ageing of wines, with Pinot Blanc, Pinot Gris and Pinot Noir. His Pinot Noir is also vinified in an open maceration cuve from Burgundy, kept on the skins for 15 days. In 1987, he has also produced a small quantity of *vin de paille*, a great speciality of the region in former times. As he himself says, he would be bored if he just continued making wines exactly in the manner of his forefathers.

JULIEN RIEFFEL, MITTLEBERGHEIM

The Rieffel family have eight hectares of vineyards in the region of Mittlebergheim. The wines are vinified in their beautiful old cellars, which date – like much of the village – back to the end of the sixteenth century, and are built into the limestone rock of the surrounding vineyards. Space is at a premium here and the press is housed immediately above the cellars, grapes being pumped up into the press, or fork-lifted in the case of grapes for their Crémant, the appellation stipulating that grapes must be put whole into the press for this wine. Fermentation is mainly in wood and temperature control was fitted to the traditional casks three years ago, giving their wines a finer bouquet, although they now take longer to evolve. Their best vineyard sites are a small area of Grand Cru

Kirchberg and a part of the famous Zotzenberg vineyard, formerly known for its superb Sylvaner, but now created a Grand Cru site and therefore moving increasingly to plantations of Riesling and Gewurztraminer. Most of Rieffel's wines are sold to private clients, although a small amount is exported to Belgium, Holland and Germany.

DOMAINE SCHLUMBERGER, GUEBWILLER

The Schlumberger vineyards are still family-owned and comprise 140 hectares, of which 70 hectares are on Grand Cru vineyards. This is the largest single holding of Grand Cru and there are few vines around the town of Guebwiller which are not part of the *domaine*. In fact, unlike most of the other towns in Alsace, there are only three growers in Guebwiller, the other two of whom own four to five hectares apiece. Ernest Schlumberger was largely responsible for the size and quality of their vineyards, having had the foresight in the early part of this century to buy up land and to plant it with the noble varieties. He was one of the pioneers of quality viticulture at that time when the argument for the continued use of hybrids was so strong. *Domaine* Schlumberger employs 40 full-time workers of the vineyards, with over a hundred at vintage time, when 800 kilometres of picking is carried out over a period of 6 weeks. The press-house is understandably immense, to cope with the volume of grapes and comprises a mixture of presses from two old Colin horizontal presses with chains, the first of their type, through to the modern Willmes pneumatic press. The juice is centrifuged to clear impurities and then fermented either in wood or in stainless steel. Where necessary, temperature control is effected by chilling part of the must in a chiller tank. An underground stream runs through the cellars, keeping them cool and moist. The Grand Cru wines are kept for one to two years in cask before bottling, to evolve the wines. The scale of production is mind-boggling and the number of different wines per year comparatively few for the size of the operation. Schlumberger are aiming at the quality sector of the market, as can be seen from their average yield over the past ten years of only 47 hectolitres per hectare.

JEAN SIPP, RIBEAUVILLÉ

Jean Sipp and his son Jean Jacques run this 20 hectare *domaine*, which includes six hectares of the Grand Cru Kirchberg. Production is traditional and grapes are pressed in a Vaslin press, the wines being vinified in wood and in glass-lined tanks. The vines are between 25 and 35 years old, giving good depth and intensity to the wines, which are vinified to keep a small amount of residual sugar, between four and five grammes. 20 per cent of the production is sold to the endless stream of tourists passing through the town and a large reception bar is fitted up to cater for the numbers of visitors. Jean Sipp produce a range of eaux-de-vie in addition to their wines.

F. E. TRIMBACH, RIBEAUVILLÉ

The Trimbach family have been winemakers in Alsace since 1626. In 1898, Frédéric Emile Trimbach, after whom the company is named, showed his wines in the International Show in Brussels, winning the highest awards. Today the company is run by Hubert and Bernard Heydt-Trimbach – Hubert looking after the commercial interests and Bernard the winemaking. In addition to the family-owned vineyards, Trimbach buy in grapes from around 50 growers. There is a preliminary selection of the grapes on arrival, according to oechsle, or sugar content, and the grapes are then pressed, using Vaslin presses. Only the first pressing is used for Trimbach's wines and the juice is centrifuged, before fermentation in glass-lined tanks, at between 20° and 25°C. Bernard believes that a lower temperature would change the character of his wines and would not be so good for their long-term development. After bottling, the Réserve wines are kept for at least a year, and the best cuvées for three to four years, to avoid the wines being released onto the market and drunk whilst still in their infancy. Trimbach keep back one of the largest stocks of wine in the region. Their top cuvée, Clos Sainte Hune, is a Riesling from a small vineyard in Hunawihr, in the heart of the Grand Cru Rosacker. This is their own vineyard and produces an average of around 700 cases a year. Their other de luxe cuvées, Riesling Frédéric Emile and Gewurztraminer Seigneurs de Ribeaupierre, are also produced from their own vines.

The house style of Trimbach is elegant and restrained, with intense fruit and great finesse and purity. Even the Vendange Tardive wines, produced occasionally in top vintages, are of the leaner, less opulent style and their best wines are capable of very long ageing.

CAVE VINICOLE DE TURCKHEIM

This top co-operative was founded in 1955 and members own 280 hectares, with an additional 100 hectares under contract for wine delivery. The holdings cover some very prestigious vineyard sites, including parts of Grand Crus Brand, Hengst, Sommerberg and Ollwiller. The annual production is between 25,000 and 30,000 hectolitres, with a total stock capacity of some 52,000 hectolitres in bulk and two million bottles.

Their wines are marketed under the Mayerling, Woellfelin, Baron de Turckheim and Decapole labels, as well as under the Cave de Turckheim label. An anomaly of French law permits the words *Propriétaires Récoltants* to appear on the label because the members of the co-operative are individual growers. Thirty five per cent of their production is from Chasselas, Sylvaner and Pinot Blanc, the majority of 65 per cent coming from the finer varieties: Riesling, Muscat, Tokay, Gewurztraminer and Pinot Noir, the latter being oak-aged. The co-operative also produces Crément d'Alsace and eaux-de-vie. In good vintages excellent Vendange Tardive wines are produced.

The accent throughout is on quality, and I have found all their wines very reliable.

DOMAINE ZIND HUMBRECHT, WINTZENHEIM

The *Domaine* Zind Humbrecht commenced in 1959, with the marriage of Léonard Humbrecht to Géneviève Zind and the subsequent merging of their vineyards. The Humbrechts had two-and-a-half hectares in Gueberschwihr and the Zinds four hectares in Wintzenheim. Before this date, both families had made and sold their own wines. In fact, there have been

Humbrechts in Alsace for a very long time and the family has been growing vines since 1620. Canon Barth, a historian of the Alsace region, records that the Humbrecht family were tenants of vineyards belonging to the Abbey of Marbach, near Gueberschwihr, in the eighteenth century, but it was only after 1947 that they started making and selling their own wines, which had always previously been sold through *négociants*.

Léonard Humbrecht had worked in various vineyard regions as an apprentice, or *stageur*, in his youth, and had previously thought of selling up and leaving Alsace, but on his marriage he decided to remain. He and his wife built cellars in Wintzenheim in 1959. In the 1960s the market for Alsace wines was somewhat depressed and wines and vineyards sold cheaply. It was not a good market in which to start trading. Léonard Humbrecht acquired more vineyard land in the 1970s, bringing his holdings to 30 hectares, spread over the communes of Thann, Turckheim, Wintzenheim, Gueberschwihr, Hattstatt and Pfaffenheim. These include parcels of the Grand Cru vineyards of Rangen, Hengst, Brand and Goldert.

Léonard Humbrecht is a perfectionist: the grapes produced on each piece of land are vinified separately, to bring out the full potential of the grape and the soil type. Vines are planted in a higher than usual density, from 5,000 vines per hectare, to six or seven thousand vines per hectare on newer plantations, to persuade each vine to produce less and thus more concentrated wine. From 1986 the vines are pressed in a pneumatic press, to give a cleaner juice, and the yield from the *domaine* averages between 35 and 50 hectolitres per hectare.

His son, Olivier, looks set to follow in the family footsteps. He has just completed a thesis on the influence of soil on the aromatics of wine, in which he has taken an in-depth look at soil structures and depth, root structure, the effect of slope and temperature of soil on the wine produced. He has also made four different cuvées of Sélection de Grains Nobles, which are amongst the most concentrated wines of their kind ever to be produced. The entire range, from these rarities down to his simple Pinot Blanc, is produced with the same meticulous care and attention to detail which marks a very great winemaker.

SOME VINEYARDS

BRAND, TURCKHEIM

Legend has it that the sun fought a battle with a dragon on these slopes, forcing it to retreat into a distant cave. The name means 'burnt soil' and the soil is of black granite and mica, with coarse sand topsoil, rich in minerals such as phosphate, potassium and magnesium. The lower slopes have a deeper topsoil of sand and silt. As the vine roots can suffer from lack of water in a dry vintage unless they extend deep into the subsoil, wines from Brand are often better in wetter vintages, and they age more rapidly than other Grand Cru wines because of relatively low acidity and high alcohol. Brand is an excellent vineyard for Riesling and has been cited since the Middle Ages as the best vineyard in Turckheim.

HATSCHBOURG, VOEGTLINSHOFFEN

The vineyard of Hatschbourg was granted Grand Cru status in 1983. It is a large vineyard of 47·36 hectares, between Voegtlinshoffen and Hattstatt, made up of a heavy limestone marl subsoil, with a stony limestone topsoil. It is a very sheltered site, with low rainfall, which produces heavy, rich wines, full-bodied and strong in alcohol. It is a particularly good site for Gewurztraminer and Tokay-Pinot Gris, producing wines with a strong earthy flavour. It has long been known as one of the best vineyard sites in Alsace. In the thirteenth century Augustine monks praised the wines of the monastic vineyards as Voegtlinshoffen and in the sixteenth and seventeenth centuries title deeds show that the wines from this vineyard fetched very high prices. In 1929 Voegtlinshoffen won a diploma as the 'Model Vineyard' from the association of viticulteurs of Alsace and today it is still one of the leading sites in the region.

KASTELBERG, GRAND CRU CLASSÉ

The vineyard of Kastelberg, overlooking the village of Andlau in the Bas Rhin, covers an area of 5·82 hectares. The soil is of schist de Steige, and is unique in Alsace. It is the oldest geological formation in the region, with stony soil over rocky subsoil, sloping sharply at an angle of up to 45°. The soil character imparts a very intense, gunflint aroma and taste to the wines. The Riesling, the only variety authorised for this site, has a distinct, steely power, needing many years to reach its peak. Vines have been grown on Kastelberg since Roman times. Archives dated 1064 proclaim that Kastelberg was the greatest vineyard in the region.

The vineyard is too steep to be worked mechanically, all weeding, spraying, pruning and picking having to be done by hand, and at the time of picking, heavy hods full of grapes have to be hauled up the slope on the picker's back. Rain causes erosion of the retaining walls, which also have to be repaired by hand. Every few years, the pH, which is low, has to be raised by the addition of chalk. Although the vineyard is rich in mineral matter, it is low in nitrogenous matter, which is supplied by herbage.

Whimpheling, a famous preacher in Renaissance times, wrote that the wines of Andlau and Kayserberg were worth more in wooden or clay cups than the wines of Zorn or Kochersberg in golden goblets, and the wines of Kastelberg still rank today amongst the finest of all Alsace.

KITTERLÉ

The vineyard of Kitterlé, to the north of Guebwiller, at the foot of the Lauch valley, covers an area of 25·79 hectares, and was created a Grand Cru in 1983. The soil is of a pinkish sandstone, with quartz gravel, rich in siliceous iron, and the slope forms a part of the Massif of Unterlingen. The Kitterlé vineyard has been renowned for generations and mentions can be found in literature since 1699. A part of the vineyard has belonged to the Jesuits of Eguisheim since 1782. According to Fidelis, 'the white wines from Kitterlé reached up to 12·2° between 1859 and 1862', a high degree for the times. At the beginning of this century, the slopes of Kitterlé were practically unplanted and its present reputation owes much to the efforts of Ernest Schlumberger, who bought up and planted the vineyard as plots fell vacant. Today the firm of Schlumberger own by far the largest holdings of Kitterlé, which is planted mainly with Riesling and Gewurztraminer, with some Tokay-Pinot Gris, which produced a Grand Cru wine on this site for the first time in 1985. The vineyard is not suited to Muscat grapes, but the other three Grand Cru varietals produce probably Schlumberger's best wines, with the longest staying power and the most potential.

RANGEN DE THANN, GRAND CRU CLASSÉ

The Rangen vineyard is the most southerly Grand Cru vineyard, in the commune of Thann. It has always enjoyed a wide reputation and has many mentions throughout history. In 1468 Charles the Bold and his Burgundians came to Thann and a chronicler of the time records that the local wine was very popular. After their visit there was a saying of the region that no man, save a Burgundian, could drink a pot of Rang-wein without forthwith rolling under the table. The wine at this time is recorded to have been made from the Gentil grape. Jullien also mentions the strength of the wine, which '*attaque les nerfs avec une telle violence, que ceux qui en usent avec excès sont, quelques temps après, comme paralysés*'. In the sixteenth century Rangen was known for its Muscat and Traminer. In 1905 Herzog recorded that the area was mostly planted with common varieties such as Burger or Rheinleben, Gutedel and a little Olber. Now the vineyards are planted with Riesling, Tokay and Gewurztraminer, producing some of the finest, most powerful wines of Alsace. The delimited vineyard covers an area of 18·41 hectares, on steeply sloping hillsides, planted in terraces. The topsoil is thin, on a base of volcanic rocks, with silica and lava base, unique in Alsace. The slopes, sometimes up to 68°, look down on the Thur river, which flows at the foot of the vineyard, helping to prevent spring frosts. The wines of Rangen are characterised by a marked *goût de terroir* – earthy, broad, strongly flavoured, and capable of very long ageing.

There is still a local saying 'que le Rangen te heurte' – 'may you be hit by the Rangen', or 'may the devil strike you dead'.

The wine enjoys the reputation which it has always had, of a wine to be drunk in moderation.

CLOS SAINTE HUNE

The vineyard of Clos Sainte Hune, which belongs to the Trimbach family, is in the heart of the Rosacker vineyard, overlooking the village of Hunawihr. It has belonged to the family for about two hundred years, and its limestone chalk soil, made up of the skeletons of millions of long-dead sea creatures, is an ideal base for the Riesling vines planted there. The vines, averaging around twenty-two years old, are planted 1·4 metres square, and the yield is carefully controlled, not just by tight pruning, but by removing some of the grape bunches after setting, in mid-July to mid-August. The crop may be reduced by up to a third in this way, allowing the remaining bunches to gain the maximum in concentration and flavour. The vineyard, a mere 1·25 hectares in size, only produces around 600 cases a year, and sometimes in difficult vintages, such as 1977, far less, around 250/300 cases. In some years all the wine is de-classified by the Trimbach family, and is blended into their Riesling Reserve, so that in vintages such as 1984, 1980 and 1972 there was no Clos Sainte Hune at all. The average yield is under 50 hectolitres per hectare and the wine is never released until it has had several years' ageing. It is a wine that needs time, young vintages can appear somewhat hard and closed, but it has unsurpassed ageing potential and older, mature vintages can be a revelation.

SCHOENENBOURG, RIQUEWIHR

The Schoenenbourg vineyard, which was created Grand Cru in 1985, is a steeply-sloping hillside to the north of Riquewihr. When the original list was drawn up in 1983, Schoenenbourg was excluded, as the vignerons were not united in wishing for the appellation, with its restrictions on varieties planted and smaller yields. It is an excellent site for the Riesling grape, south-facing, very steep, with a light, well-aerated, sandy, stony topsoil and a clay, gypsum subsoil, with keuper marl and Vosges sandstone. The subsoil is fertile and has good water

retention in dry vintages. Schoenenbourg Rieslings are generally quite full-flavoured, powerful, firm wines, with their
acidity often masked by the weight of fruit.

GRAND CRU WIEBELSBERG, ANDLAU

The Grand Cru vineyard of Wiebelsberg is actually almost a
continuation of the Kastelberg vineyard to the east, overlooking the village of Andlau. Its soil, however, is very different,
the two slopes having been formed by various geological
upheavals which pushed the two formations against each
other, so the Wiebelsberg vineyard is made up of a Vosges
sandstone subsoil, with light, almost sandy topsoil, which is
very well-drained and reflects the warmth of the sun onto the
vines. Wiebelsberg is not as steeply sloping as Kastelberg,
although it is still quite steep, around 30°, and the vines are
grown at an altitude of between 250 and 300 metres above sea
level. The area of 10·32 hectares faces south and south-west,
and is mainly planted with Riesling, although small plantations of Tokay and Muscat may be found. Generally the
wines from Wiebelsberg are gentle, flowery and almost spicy.
Less blockbusting than some, they nevertheless have good
ageing potential and retain their lightness and charm for many
years. The vineyard was already considered as 'Grand Cru'
quality when Stoltz wrote his *Ampelography of Alsace* in 1852.

ZOTZENBERG

The Zotzenberg vineyard, north-west of Mittelbergheim, has
long been cited as producing the best Sylvaners in Alsace. In a
warm vintage, such as 1983, the Sylvaners from this vineyard
have a wonderful spicy richness. Unfortunately, there is not
much money in producing wonderful Sylvaner, and as the
vineyard was upgraded to Grand Cru in 1985, many growers
are busy replacing the Sylvaner vines with Riesling or
Gewurztraminer. Sylvaner, not being a Grand Cru variety,
would no longer be able to use the word Zotzenberg once the
vineyard has been fully delimited. At present, growers can
choose: Grand Cru varieties can either be labelled 'Gewurztraminer Grand Cru Zotzenberg', undergo the extra tasting

tests and observe the smaller yield laid down under Grand Cru regulations, or they can be labelled 'Gewurztraminer Zotzenberg', as they were before Grand Cru was granted. In this case they do not need to observe the Grand Cru requirements. Once the committees have drawn up the definitive vineyard plan, delimiting the area and the boundaries of the Grand Cru, the name will only be allowed for wines that comply fully with the legislation. Growers are petitioning to be allowed to retain the vineyard name for their Sylvaners, on the grounds that this vineyard has a very long history of association with this variety, but it is unlikely to be allowed. Zotzenberg, on the slopes of the Rippelsholz, is made up of a very complex soil, formed of jurassic marl to the west and sandstone and limestone to the east. Further up the vineyard at around 320 metres there is a thin, stony, limestone topsoil, with good water retention and this is the area of the best wines. Lower down the slope, where the topsoil is deeper and more alluvial, the wines show less character. The best wines from this vineyard have very good ageing potential.

THE CONFRÉRIE ST-ÉTIENNE

The Confrérie originated in the fourteenth century, as an association of important citizens, in the town of Ammerschwihr. From 1561 one of their duties was to control the quality of the local wines. In 1951 the society became regional rather than local and their function is to promote interest in the wines of Alsace. Each year they hold tastings to award the Confrérie seal. The wines are judged in their second year and must be typical of the vintage and variety. The *Sigille de Qualité* is valid for two years only from this date, wines must be re-submitted after that. The Confrérie also hold dinners each year, both in Alsace and abroad, to introduce people to the wines of Alsace. New members have to pass a simple tasting test, to identify the wines of the region, before admittance. In order to avoid jealousy or accusations of favouritism, wines at Confrérie functions are always labelled with the Confrérie label, showing the vintage and variety, but not the producer, whose name is known only to the committee who chose and labelled the wine.

Not all growers submit their wines to the Confrérie, and there are a great many top quality wines which have never sought seals, either from the Confrérie or from other wine shows, but wines labelled with the Confrérie seal are usually very sound and reliable.

OTHER WINE SHOWS, WINE SEALS

Many towns in Alsace hold annual shows, or fairs, where the public can come and taste the wines of all the local producers. The dates for these can be found at the end of the book. In addition to the public fairs, there are also wine judgings, to which producers can submit their wines, in the hope of a gold, silver or bronze medal. The Concours at Colmar is probably the best. Wines are also often submitted to judgings outside the region, in shows such as Mâcon, Paris and Bordeaux. Wine magazines and societies also often hold 'best of the year' competitions. It is a poor wine indeed that cannot win some sort of medal somewhere and one should enquire more closely into the provenance of the medal before becoming over-impressed with a beautiful array of neck seals and medallions.

WINE FAIRS

April	Foire aux Vins, Ammerschwihr
May	Foire aux Vins, Guebwiller
	Foire Régionale aux Vins, Molsheim
	Rabseppifascht, Wine Fair, Voegtlinshoffen
June	Rabseppifascht, Foire aux Vins, Voegtlinshoffen
July	Foire aux Vins, Dambach-la-Ville
	Fête de la Fontaine à Vins, Wangen
	Foire aux Vins, Barr
	Fête du Riesling, Riquewihr
	Foire aux Vins, Ribeauvillé
August	Foire aux Vins, Turckheim
	Foire aux Vins, Colmar
	Foire aux Vins, Selestat
	Fête du Vin, Dambach-la-Ville
	Foire aux Vins, Bennwihr
	Fête de l'Amitié 'Portes et Caves Ouvertes', Gueberschwihr
September	Fête du Vin Nouveau, Riquewihr
October	Fête des Vendanges, Barr
	Foire aux Vins, Wintzenheim
	Fête des Vendanges, Obernai
	Fête des Vendanges, Marlenheim
	Grande Fête du Raisin 'Portes et Caves Ouvertes', Molsheim

BIBLIOGRAPHY

Loire, Alsace & Champagne, Hubrecht Duijker, Mitchell Beazley, London, 1983

Choose Your Wine, T. Layton, Duckworth, London, 1949

General Viticulture, Winkler etc., University of California Press Berkeley/London/Los Angeles, 1974

Topographie de Tous les Vignobles Connu, André Jullien, 1866

Histoire de la Vigne et du Vin de France, Roger Dion, Flammarion, Paris, 1977

Vines, Grapes and Wines, Jancis Robinson, Mitchell Beazley, London, 1986

Alsace Wines, Pamela Vandyke-Price, Sotheby Publications, London, 1984

La Cuisine Alsacienne, Pierre Gaertner et Robert Frederic, Flammarion, Paris, 1979

Le Grand Livre du Foie Gras, Hugues Robert Editions Daniel Briand/Robert Laffont, Toulouse, 1982

Etude des Vignobles de France, Guyot, 1876

Terroirs & Vins d'Alsace, Sittler, Sciences Géologiques, Strasbourg, 1981

Bulletin de la Societé Industrielle de Mulhouse, Le Vin d'Alsace, Mulhouse, 1981

Vignes, Vignerons et Vins d'Alsace, Editions Alsatia, Colmar, 1975

800 Ans de Viticulture en Haute-Alsace, Maurice Boesch, Imprimerie Art'Real, Guebwiller, 1983

Monseigneur le Vin, Nicolas

Wines of the World 1875, Vizetelli

Dictionnaire des Appellations de Tous les Vins de France, Fernand Woutaz, Marabout, Alleuf Belgium, 1986

Guide des Vins d'Alsace, Guy Renvoise, Solarama, 1983

Terroirs et Vins de France, Charles Pomerol Total Edition Presse, Paris, 1984

Wines and People of Alsace, T. A. Layton Cassell, London, 1970

A History and Description of Modern Wines, C. Redding, 1833

INDEX

Adam, J. B., 51, 77, 86, 94, 117, 124, 133, 139, 151, 155, 168, 200, 204, 209, 215

Albrecht, Lucien, 51, 87, 124, 155, 204

Ancel, Victor, 52

Andlau, Cave Co-operative, 52, 124, 178, 204, 213

Beblenheim, Cave Co-operative, 66, 105, 144, 161, 194, 227

Beck, Gaston, 53, 94, 140, 190

Becker, J., 53, 95, 140, 155, 178, 190

Bennwihr, Cave Co-operative, 53, 156, 179, 223

Beyer, Léon, 53, 95, 125, 140, 156, 171, 179, 191, 204, **233**

Blanck, Paul/ Freres, 54, 125, 141, 156, 224

Boeckel, Emile, 55, 96, 141, 180, 191

Bott Frères, 55, 97, 125, 141, 156, 180, 224, **233**

Boxler, Albert, 56, 98, 126, 172, **234**

Brucker, F., 56, 98

Bucher, Camille, 98

Cattin, Joseph, 99, 126, 141, 157

Cattin, Théo, 99, 126, 157, 180, 191

Clos St. Landelin, 72, 111, 131, 147, **228**

Deiss, Marcel /J. M., 56, 87, 100, 127, 142, 157, 181, 191, **234**

Dirler, J. P., 58, 101, 142, 204

Dopff au Moulin, 59, 88, 127, 158, 224, **235**

Dopff Irion, 59, 88, 101, 143, 158, 172

Eguisheim, Cave Co-operative, 84, 121, 171

Ehrhart, Domaine, 59, 101, 192, 229

Eppelé, Félix, 60, 102, 159

Faller, Théo, 61, 88, 102, 128, 143, 159, 173, 192, 204, **236**

Freyberger, Louis, 61, 102

Freyermuth, Lucien, 103, 226

Gaertner, Victor, 62, 103, 143, 160, 205

Gaschy, A., 56, 98

Geschickt, Jérome, 62, 103, 129, 143, 160, 181, 192, 205, 226

Gilg, Armand, 62, 205

Ginglinger, Paul, 104

Gisselbrecht, Louis, 63, 104, 144, 160, 182, 193, 205, 227

Gisselbrecht, Willy, 63, 104, 129, 144, 161, 173, 182, 193, 206, 227

Gresser, André et Remy, 64, 104

Hellmuth, A., 65

Hering, E., 65, 193, 206

Heywang, Jean, 65, 104, 144, 206, 213, 218, **236**

Hoen, Baron de, 66, 105, 144, 161, 194, 227

Hugel et Fils, 66, 89, 107, 129, 161, 173, 182, 194, 206, 210

Humbrecht, Marcel, 66, 144, 162, 194

Ingersheim, Cave Co-operative, 195, 207

Joggerst, René, 183
Josmeyer, 67, 107, 145, 195

Kientzler, André, 67, 89, 108, 130, 145, 162, 174, 195, 210, **237**
Koeberlé-Kreyer, 162
Koehly, C., 163
Kreydenweiss, Marc, 68, 90, 108, 130, 146, 163, 174, 183, 197, 207, 227, **238**
Kuentz-Bas, 69, 108, 130, 146, 163, 183, 196

Landmann, G., 69, 207
Landmann, Ostholt, 69, 163
Laugel, Michel, 183, 228
Lorentz, J., 69, 109, 130, 197
Lorentz, Philippe, 69, 109
Lupfen, Comtes de, 54, 125, 141, 156, 224

Mader, J.-L., 70, 183
Mallo, Frédéric, 70, 90, 109, 146, 164, 207, **239**
Meckert, René, 213
Metz, Frères, 110

Metz, Hubert, 70, 110, 147, 184
Mittnacht, Paul, 228
Mochel, Frédéric, 71, 110, 147
Muller, J., 72, 110, 131, 164, 198
Muré, 72, 111, 131, 147, 164, 175, 184, 228

Obrecht, 218
Ostertag, Domaine, 72, 111, 132, 147, 164, 184, 198, 207, **239**
Ostheimer-Boersch, 111

Pfaffenheim, Cave Co-operative, 111
Pfister, Veuve J., 77, 117, 133, 151, 168, 200, 209
Pfluger-Haegel, 73, 112, 148, 165, 208, 219
Preiss, Henny, 73
Preiss, Victor, 112
Preiss Zimmer, 73, 112, 149, 165
Princes de Terroir, 113

Rieffel, Julien, 74, 90, 113, 198, 208, **240**
Ritzenthaler, Pierre, 165
Roesselstein, Cave du, 219
Rolly Gassmann, 74, 113, 149, 165, 199, 219

Ruff, A., 214

Ste. Odile, Société Vinicole, 75, 114, 166
Schaetzel, M., 75, 149, 166, 200, 208
Schleret, Charles, 75, 114, 150, 166, 185
Schlumberger, Domaine, 75, 114, 132, 150, 167, 185, 200, 209, 220, **241**
Schmidt, René, 77, 115, 150, 200
Schmitt, Roland, 76, 116
Schoech, Albert, 77, 116, 151, 185, 200
Schoech, Maurice, 77, 117, 167, 186, 216, 220
Schroedel, 77, 117, 133, 151, 168, 200, 209
Schwach, Paul, 77, 118, 151, 168, 186, 201
Seltz, Alsace, 209
Seltz, Emile, 209
Sick-Dreyer, 78, 118, 168, 201, 211
Sigolsheim, Cave Co-operative, 78, 119, 169
Sipp, Jean, 78, 119, 133, 168, 187, **242**
Sipp, Louis, 79, 119, 186
Sparr, Pierre, 79, 120, 134, 151, 169, 216, 220, 228

Spener, Ph. J., 80

Thomann, J. B., 81,
120, 151, 228
Trimbach, F. E.,
81, 120, 134, 151,
169, 201, 209,
242
Turckheim, Cave
Co-operative, 82,
121, 135, 152,

170, 187, 202,
243

Wach, R., 83
Wantz, Alfred, 135,
187, 209, 221,
229
Weibel, M., 170,
187
Wiederhirn,
Maison, 83, 91,

121, 153, 170, 221
Willm, A., 84, 121,
135, 153, 221
Wolfberger, 84,
121, 171, 229

Zind Humbrecht,
Domaine, 85, 91,
121, 136, 153,
171, 175, 188,
202, **243**